RESOLUTION OF TAX TREATY CONFLICTS BY ARBITRATION

47th IFA Congress
Florence 1993

RESOLUTION OF TAX TREATY CONFLICTS BY ARBITRATION

Proceedings of a Seminar held in Florence, Italy
in 1993 during the 47th Congress of the
International Fiscal Association

Vol. 18e

KLUWER LAW AND TAXATION PUBLISHERS
DEVENTER – BOSTON

Kluwer Law and Taxation Publishers
P.O. Box 23 Tel. : 31-5700-47261
7400 GA Deventer Telex : 49295
The Netherlands Fax : 31-5700-22244

ISBN 90 6544 8683

RESOLUTION OF TAX TREATY CONFLICTS BY ARBITRATION*

Proceedings of a Seminar held in Florence, Italy, in 1993 during the 47th Congress of the International Fiscal Association

---

Chairman of the Seminar:
Professor Gustaf Lindencrona (Sweden)
University of Stockholm

Panelists:
Dr. Alfred E. Burckhardt (Switzerland)
Oeri & Partner, Basel

Professor Mario Burgio (Italy)
Principal Administrator, European Commission, Brussels
Professor of European Tax Law at the College of Europe in Bruges

Professor Luc Hinnekens (Belgium)
Lawyer, Baker & McKenzie, Brussels

Professor William W. Park (USA)
Boston University; Counsel, Ropes & Gray, Boston; Vice President, London Court of International Arbitration

Professor Wolfgang Ritter (Germany)
BASF Aktiengesellschaft, Ludwigshafen

Secretary:
Dr. Guiseppe Marino (Italy)
Studio Uckmar, Milan

* *The views expressed are those of the authors and not necessarily those of the International Fiscal Association*

IFA CONGRESS SEMINAR SERIES*

1. Work in Intergovernmental Organizations on Transnational Companies (Congress 1976) (out of print)

2. The Revised OECD Model Double Taxation Convention on Income and Capital (Congress 1977) (out of print)

3. Fiscal Policy and Tax Structures in the Pacific Region (Congress 1978) (out of print)

4. UN Draft Model Taxation Convention (Congress 1979) (out of print)

5. Recourse to Tax Havens – Use and Abuse (Congress 1980) (out of print)

6. Taxation of the Income Arising from the International Seabed (Congress 1981)

7. Imputation Systems – Objectives and Consequences (Congress 1982)

8. Tax Policy towards the National Heritage (Congress 1983)

9. Adjustments for Tax Purposes in Highly Inflationary Economies (Congress 1984)

10. International Tax Problems of Charities and other Private Institutions with similar Tax Treatment (Congress 1985)

11a. Taxation of domestic shareholders on undistributed income of foreign corporate affiliates: objectives, technique and consequences (Congress 1986)

* Available from Kluwer Law and Taxation Publishers
P.O. Box 23
7400 GA Deventer, The Netherlands
(tel.: +31 5700 47261 – fax +31 5700 22244)

11b. International Tax Treatment of Common Law Trusts (Congress 1986)

12. Taxation and Human Rights (Congress 1987)

13a. Data Processing in Taxation (Congress 1988)

13b. Tax Consequences of Pension Provision for the Internationally Transferred Employee (Congress 1988)

Draft EC directives on parent-subsidiary, on mergers and on arbitration (Congress 1988)**

14a. International Taxation of Services (Congress 1989)

14b. Tax Treaties and Domestic Legislation (Congress 1989)

15. Double Taxation Treaties between Industrialised and Developing Countries; OECD and UN Models, a Comparison (Congress 1990)

16. Tax Treaties and Local Taxes (Congress 1991)

17a. Advance Ruling: Practice and Legality (Congress 1992)

18c. Corporate Tax on Distributions (Equalization Tax) (Congress 1993)

18e. Resolution of Tax Treaty Conflicts by Arbitration (Congress 1993)

** Available from the International Bureau of Fiscal Documentation, P.O. Box 20237, 1000 HE Amsterdam, The Netherlands, tel.: +31 206267726 – fax: +31 206228658.

TABLE OF CONTENTS

FOREWORD

This book contains articles by some of the panelists of Seminar E on the subject 'Resolution of tax treaty conflicts by arbitration' on the Congress of the International Fiscal Association in Florence on Thursday, 7 October 1993. The contents of the articles is related to the speeches made by the panelists during the Seminar but is generally much wider in scope.

Gustaf Lindencrona
Chairman of the Seminar

RECENT DEVELOPMENT OF TAX TREATY ARBITRATION

Professor Gustaf Lindencrona

Background

The International Fiscal Association has since a long time ago been interested in various solutions for solving disputes in the international tax field.

These matters were discussed at length at the fifth Congress of the Organization in Zurich in 1951, where one of the topics was 'Judicial Interpretation of Conventions on Double Taxation and the necessity or advisability of establishing an International Fiscal Jurisdiction'.

The Congress adopted a resolution, in which was recommended 'the creation, under the auspices of the most qualified international groups, of a permanent juridical committee which would have as its aim to bring to the attention of the Fiscal Committee of the UN, the claims presented to them which appear well founded and to inform the interested governments'.

The inclusion in multilateral conventions of a 'clause envisaging the institution of mixed commissions between the two states to solve certain cases of double taxation' and of 'an obligatory arbitration clause permitting the contracting States to have determined by an arbitrator the meaning of the clause under dispute' was also recommended.

Unfortunately, the discussions at the IFA's fifth Congress in Zurich and the resolutions adopted after the discussion did not lead directly to any concrete result. However, the debate continued, and the standpoint adopted by the IFA played an important part in the debate.

In the 1957 and 1960 IFA Congresses in Vienna and Basel, respectively, the question of international tax courts was raised once again.

One of the two topics at the Basel Congress, the forteenth Congress, was 'The Interpretation of the Double Taxation Conventions'. The main interest was concentrated on the mutual agreement procedure, but the resolution contained references to the explicit need of international tax courts.

More recently the question of conflict solution in the tax field was discussed at the IFA Congress in Berlin, when the topic was 'Mutual agreements – procedure and practice' and at a seminar at the Congress in Brussels in 1987 'Effectiveness of current competent authority procedures for relief of double taxation'. At both occasions arbitration was discussed.

Even if IFA was the first international organization to take up in its program the questions of conflict solutions in the area of international tax law the idea has been promoted by other organizations as well. The World Association of Lawyers supported the arbitration idea at its Congress in Madrid in 1979 and especially the objectives and proposals of the Lindencrona-Mattsson study (later published as 'Arbitration in taxation'). The International Chamber of Commerce has devoted much work to the question of the resolution of international tax conflicts. A document promoting the idea or arbitration in tax conflicts was adopted in 1984. The International Chamber of Commerce has since then vigorously promoted the arbitration idea.

In the last years we have seen a breakthrough of the arbitration idea. Most important is the agreement by the Member States of the European Community in 1990 on a convention for the elimination of double taxation in connection with the adjustment of transfers of profits between association enterprises (arbitration procedure). Other important recent events have been the inclusion of an arbitration clause in some important double taxation conventions.

The recent developments have actualized the principal and practical questions of arbitration in taxation.

Recent Solutions adopted

In this article I will give a summary of recent development in tax treaty arbitration. Provisions for arbitration have been included in several tax treaties. As the treaties are so new and in some cases not ratified there have not been any cases this far. I must therefore base my article on the text of the treaties and other documents. The technique of international tax arbitration has been developed in another context with the Apple case in the United States. This case is analysed in the article by professor Park. After the description of recent developments I will make some comments on some controversial questions in the future development of tax treaty arbitration.

Arbitration clauses have to date been introduced in the German-Swedish, the German-French, the US-German, the US-Mexican and the US-Dutch double taxation treaties. The most important treaty is, however, the EC Arbitration Convention. The texts of the provisions can be found in the appendices.

Summary of the Treaty Provisions

The insertion of an arbitration provision in five important treaties and in the EC Arbitration Convention is a major breakthrough of the idea of arbitration in tax matters. The double taxation conventions do not, however, settle all questions. They are usually very short and contain only the most basic provisions. They must be supplemented by further regulations. This is especially important as the solution of tax treaty conflicts by arbitration in modern times is such a recent phenomenon. In fact, one of the treaties, the US-German treaty has already been supplemented by an exchange of letters in which important questions of arbitration procedure is settled in detail. It would be a misconception if the lack of such further regulations to the other treaties is regarded as if the problems did not exist or were not thought of. The reason for the difference is probably only that supplementary regulations to the other treaties are not ready.

It must be acknowledged, however, that the contracting states proceed with extreme cautiousness. If we look to the double taxation treaties in which arbitration clauses have so far been introduced we find that they have not made the arbitration procedure mandatory. Both the German-Swedish and the US-German treaty call for agreement between the parties for the conflict to be submitted to arbitration. The only difference is that the German-Swedish treaty speaks about the contracting states and the German-US treaty about the competent authorities. The additional protocol to the German-French treaty has a time limit of 24 months but still does not make arbitration mandatory. It just says that if a solution is not found within this time limit, the competent authorities may agree to invoke an arbitration commission. The US-Dutch and the US-Mexican treaty require that both competent authorities and the taxpayer or even taxpayers agree to submit the conflict to arbitration.

It is only the EC Arbitration Convention which has got a procedure that might be called mandatory. If the competent authorities have not been able to find a solution within two years thay shall submit the conflict to an advisory committee. The advisory committee should deliver its opinion within six months. The competent authorities are, however, free to reach another solution than the solution recommended by the commission. It is only if they have been unable to do so within six months that the opinion of the commission will be binding and thus can be called an arbitration award.

The position of the taxpayers is another important subject. Arbitration in tax matters is a procedure between states. It is, however, the taxpayers that have suffered and who are mainly interested in the outcome of the arbitration. The position of the taxpayers in the procedure is therefore an important question. The main questions are if the taxpayers should be able to influence the choice of arbitrators and if they should have a right to be present at the meetings of the arbitration commission.

None of the treaties have this far given the taxpayer any right to influence the choice of arbitrators. As the arbitration procedure is a procedure between states the rules are concerned with the balance between the contracting states, not between competent authorities and taxpayers. The exchange of letters between Germany and the US opens the possibility for more than three members on the arbitration board. They shall come from either contracting state or from another OECD Member State. The possibility of arbitrators nominated by the taxpayer is thus not excluded. The EC Arbitration Convention, however, expressly excludes persons who are not independent in relation to the taxpayers.

As for the possibilities to take part in the procedure the treaty provisions are much more generous to the taxpayers. The EC Arbitration Convention says that taxpayers 'may provide any information, evidence or documents' and that they may 'appear or be represented before the advisory commission'. This position is also taken in the German-Swedish treaty and the exchange of letters between Germany and the US. The other treaties lack this far detailed procedural rules. There is no reason to believe that they will not follow suit in this matter.

Arbitration in tax questions is easily introduced by the insertion of an arbitration clause in a double taxation convention. The arbitration commission could be appointed on an *ad hoc*-basis when a conflict has arisen. It could be argued, however, that the establishment of an arbitration institute with experienced arbitrators and technical services would facilitate the arbitration procedure. This is done to a certain extent in the treaties, at least in the EC Arbitration Convention which calls for the establishment of a list of independent persons of standing. Such a list will give some stability to the arbitration procedure.

The relation between the arbitration award and national tax law is complicated in some countries where even a mutual agreement sometimes cannot be implemented for constitutional and other reasons. The only solution to this problem found in the treaties is in the EC Arbitration Convention which exempts a state from participating in a mutual agreement or an arbitration procedure in such a case.

The principal source of law in an arbitration procedure is of course the double taxation convention. It could be discussed, however, if other sources could be used too, for example the Commentary to the OECD Model Convention or general principles of international tax law and previous awards. Even more important is the question to what extent the arbitrators could use the national tax law of the treaty-making states. The amending protocol to the German-French treaty mentions the rules of international law and especially the provisions of the convention. The exchange of letters to the US-German treaty says that 'the arbitration board shall decide each specific case on the basis of the Convention, giving due consideration to the domestic law of the Contracting States and the principles of international law'. The EC Arbitration Convention simply refers to Article 4 of the convention, which limits the applicability of the convention to transfer pricing questions. The more limited scope of the convention and the fact that several questions are regulated in it means that it is possible to base the decisions on the convention itself to a large degree.

The legal basis for the arbitration procedure is in all cases the double taxation treaty. It goes without saying that an award should be based on the double taxation treaty if possibly. There is no reason to exclude commonly accepted methods of treaty interpretation in arbitration cases. As the Commentary to the OECD Model Conventions has been used more and more in OECD countries there is no reason why it could not be used in arbitration cases. Countries which have ratified the Vienna Convention have also accepted its principles of interpretation. If a treaty makes reference to national law in one of the contracting states such a reference must be valid in an arbitration case too.

Finally there are several practical questions involved. In the absence of established international principles rules have to be established by the contracting states. As for US-German cases such rules have been established through the exchange of letters. The EC Arbitration Convention is also rather specific in procedural matters. It stipulates for example that the chairman shall be elected from the list of the persons of standing and must possess the qualifications required for the appointment to the highest judicial offices in his country or be a juris consultant of recognized competence.

The question of who is to bear the costs of the arbitration procedure is of course an important one. Here the basic principle established in the exchange of letters on the US-German treaty is that each contracting state shall bear its costs and that common costs shall be divided equally between the parties.

The Future of Tax Treaty Arbitration

The idea of the solution of tax treaty conflict by arbitration is thus making progress. Hopefully, many hereto unsolved problems will be solved in practice. There are, however, some more fundamental questions which will have to be answered sooner or later. I will discuss two of them; Shall arbitration be mandatory or not? and The relation between the arbitration award and national tax law.

Should Arbitration be Mandatory or not?

The discussion of arbitration as a method of solving tax treaty conflicts is based on the assumption that a preceeding mutual agreement procedure has not been successful. The taxpayer has thus applied to the competent authority in the country of which he is a resident. The competent authority has found his application justified and started negotiations with the competent authority in the other contracting state in order to find a solution. No solution has been found, however, because the competent authorities hold different views. It is also possible that there is a prospect of the competent authorities reaching an agreement, but that the procedure is extremely time-consuming.

The main difference between an arbitration procedure and a mutual agreement procedure is that the arbitration award is rendered by an independent group of arbitrators. An award should always be given. If the arbitrators cannot agree the decision is taken by a majority vote. It should also be pointed out that an arbitration award is always based on law, be it treaty provisions or general principles of international tax law. If the arbitrators try to find a solution *ex aequo et bono* it is not an arbitration procedure.

The first problem in the creation of an arbitration procedure that must be discussed is whether it should be mandatory or not. With a mandatory procedure is meant a procedure that should take place if the competent authorities are not able to reach a mutual agreement due to a difference of opinion or if the competent authorities have not been able to find a solution within a certain prescribed time limit. If the procedure is not mandatory it means that both the contracting parties must agree that an arbitration procedure should take place.

As mentioned, if we look to the double taxation tax treaties where arbitration clauses have so far been introduced, we find that thay have not made the arbitration procedure mandatory.

It is thus clear that even the states, which have been bold enough to open the possibilities of an arbitration procedure, have been very cautious an hesitated to make an arbitration procedure mandatory. There are, however, in my opinion, strong arguments for a mandatory procedure with a provision that if the parties have not been able to reach a mutual agreement within a prescribed, not too long a time, the conflict should be submitted to arbitration. The main arguments are:

1. If the arbitration procedure is not mandatory we are left with the basic problem of the mutual agreement procedure – there is no guarantee that a solution will be found in every conflict. The taxpayer is thus not ensured that double taxation will be eliminated in all cases covered by the treaty.
2. A mandatory procedure, especially if combined with a time limit, will speed up the procedure. It is a problem today that mutual agreement procedures often take too long a time.

Anyway an arbitration procedure, even if it is not mandatory, is certainly better than no arbitration procedure at all. Arbitration means that the conflict will be solved by an award and that the solution will be based on law, mainly the tax treaty.

The Relation between the Arbitration Award and National Tax

It happens that some countries feel unable to implement a mutual agreement because it is contradictory to a decision by its Supreme Court or even a court on a lower level. The same problem may occur if the conflict is solved by an arbitration award. The EC Arbitration Convention explicitly excepts a state from participating in a mutual agreement or arbitration procedure in such a case.

It is an untolerable situation that a state should be unable to participate in the solution of a tax conflict because one of its courts have reached a decision. The reason for this position is basically that the mutual agreement and the arbitration procedure is regarded as a solution of conflicts between administrative agencies, i.e. the competent authorities. It is then seen as unconstitutional that administrative agencies should be able to reach decisions that correct a court decision. The mutual agreement and the arbitration award is thus only seen as possible if there is no court decision. With this outlook it must also be avoided that the case later is taken to court, e.g. by making the taxpayer promise in writing to renounce from taking the case to court if a mutual agreement or an arbitration procedure should be initiated.

I think that no real solution to this problem can be found if the outlook of the participating states is not changed. Both the mutual agreement procedure and the arbitration procedure should be regarded as a procedure between states. The fact that the competent authorities are involved and not the diplomatic representation of the states should only be seen as a matter of practical expediency. I think that this outlook is compatible with the OECD Model Convention. The reason why Article 25 made it possible for the competent authorities to get into contact directly with one another without the use of the traditional diplomatic channels was to speed up the procedure. Taxation is also a field where technical expertise is particularily needed. Diplomats cannot be expected to possess such special knowledge. Article 25 made it possible for the tax people, who were the technical experts in the field, to speak directly with one another. The reason for Article 25 could not have been to create a possibility for conflict solution that was not fully effective. A good case for a mutual agreement or an arbitration procedure is that a treaty provision has been interpreted differently in the two contracting states. This could be done by courts as well as by tax authorities.

In my opinion the right outlook is that the fact that courts in two contracting states have interpreted a treaty differently does not in any way imply that there is something wrong with the judgements.

The reason might simply be that the courts have interpreted a treaty provision according to national definitions in a case where such an interpretation is not forbidden by the treaty. Such interpretations will, however, lead to double taxation of the taxpayer. When the contracting states after a mutual agreement or even more an arbitration award implement the agreement or award it should in no way be seen as a correction of the decision by the court. Instead the outlook should be that the state has renounced from a sum of money in order to fulfil its obligation according to international law, i.e. to make sure that it fulfils its treaty obligations.

Bibliography

Avery Jones, John F., 'The legal nature of the mutual agreement procedure under OECD Model convention', London, Sweet & Maxwell, 1979. Reprint from *British Tax Review*, No. 6, 1979, No. 1, 1980.

Broke, Adam, '1992 an International Bank taxation' in *EC Brief*, No. 6, April 1989.

International Fiscal Association (IFA), *South Asia Regional Conference 18th-20th February 1988, New Delhi, India, Background papers.* New Delhi, Vigyan Bhawan, New Delhi 1100001, India, 1988.

Klein, Klaus-Gunter, 'Die steuerlichte Verrechnungspreisgestaltung international tatiger Unternehmungen. Probleme der nationalen und internationale Anwendung des dealing-at-arm's-length-Prinzips', 1988, Steuer, *Wirtschaft und Recht,* Band 41.

Lindencrona, Gustaf, Mattsson, Nils, *Arbitration in Taxation,* Deventer, Kluwer, 1981.

Maktouf, Lofti, 'Resolving international tax disputes through arbitration', London, *London Court of International Arbitration,* Vol. 4, No. 1, January 1988.

Sass, G., 'Effectiveness of current competent authority procedures for relief on International double taxation: future developments', Deventer, Kluwer, 4 April 1988, pp. 111 – 113. *Intertax,* bimonthly.

Scholsem, J. Cl., 'The Proposal for a Council Directive on the elimination of double taxation (arbitration procedure)', in *Intertax,* No. 11 – 12, Nov.-Dec. 1982, pp. 424 – 435.

Shakow, David J., 'Confronting the problem of tax arbitrage', No. 1, Fall 1987, pp. 1 – 50, *Tax Law Review,* bimonthly.

Shoup, Carl, S., International Arbitration of transfer pricing disputes under income taxation. Centre for international business studies, Halifax, Dalhouse University, 1983.

Wehrli, Daniel, *'New Swiss law on international arbitration'*, in International Business Lawyer, Vol. 17, No. 4, April 1989, pp. 165 – 167, London, International Bar Association.

Wolfswinkel, M., 'De mutual agreement procedure nader beschouwd', Deventer, Kluwer, 118, No. 5881, September 1989, pp. 1003 – 1010, *Weekblad voor Fiscaal Recht,* weekly.

LEGAL SOURCES AND INTERPRETATION OF EUROPEAN TAX ARBITRATION CONVENTION AND ITS RECOGNITION OF THE TAXPAYER

Professor Luc Hinnekens

A. The Legal Issues

International tax arbitration opens new and important prospects for resolving tax disputes between States concerning avoidance of international double taxation and possibly other tax disputes relating to tax discrimination, interpretation of tax treaty terms, treaty abuse, (extra-)territorial tax jurisdiction, etc.

It also raises new and very basic legal questions. We examine two such general issues.

The first one deals with sources of international tax arbitration law, their relationships and interpretation. Is such arbitration governed exclusively by the treaty instituting it? Or are the treaty provisions amplified and, in case of conflict, superseded by the provisions of the domestic laws of the States concerned, of their other ordinary or Community treaties, and of General International Law? Our search for the legal rules relates to the substantive principles governing international tax arbitration, but even more to its applicable procedures.

The questions are of direct interest to the taxpayer, as the dispute is about his (double) taxation. Depending on the allocation of his income to the legislative tax jurisdiction of the one or the other State, he becomes subject to a lower or a higher tax, even if his double taxation is eliminated. Does the international procedure satisfy the procedural fairness to which the taxpayer is entitled because of this legitimate interest? Is international arbitration a second string to his bow? Or rather a second bow, as the international and the national procedures are governed by different principles and procedural rules, and risk to produce different, contradictory decisions. The situation of conflicting or incongruous results at the arbitral and domestic jurisdictional level is conceptually not very satisfactory from a viewpoint of legal certainty and consistency. Or does the international arbitration procedure exclude the application of the domestic relief procedure? In such case the taxpayer's concern for the fairness of the arbitral proceedings and his legal protection becomes even greater.

The questions lead to our second basic legal issue: what is the legal position of the taxpayer in international arbitration? Are only the States party to the procedure, or does it include (and how?) the taxpayer? If he is not a party proper to the international procedure, shouldn't he be entitled to special procedural protection and active participation?

Our second legal issue is not strictly related to the first one, except that the recognition of the taxpayer's position is determined according to all applicable legal sources and their interpretation, and in the light of the availability of other methods for resolving his tax complaint. Sources international tax arbitration law, their interlinkage and interpretation form our general legal debate; thereafter we apply its conclusions to the specific problem of the taxpayer's legal position under such arbitration law.

The legal framework of international tax arbitration is not very articulate when it comes to defining principles, procedures, relationships with concurrent jurisdictional remedies, legal sources, rights and obligations of the taxpayer and of the competent authorities. Those legal questions are no less a matter of great importance. The legal framework and the definition of the taxpayer's legal position determine the jurisdictional merits of international tax arbitration from a practical and principal standpoint.

The aforementioned legal issues of international tax arbitration are not resolved in an abstract or uniform manner, but depend on the terms of the particular international instrument that instituted it. Multilateral mandatory arbitration of cases of double taxation of profits of associated enterprises of different States has obviously a better chance of being instituted and regulated under the laws of a Community or Union of States. Especially if such (European) Community or Union recognizes very expressly the need ('that double taxation is likely to cause distortions in the conditions of competition and in capital movements and therefore to affect the operation of the common market' Preamble to Proposal for an EC-Council Directive of 29 November 1976), and provides for the means to coordinate or pool the sovereign executive fiscal jurisdiction rights of its member States.

A cornerstone of international tax arbitration is therefore the European Convention on the Elimination of Double Taxation in Connection with the Adjustment of Profits of Associated Enterprises. The Convention was signed by the plenipotentiaries of the EC-Member States, meeting within the EC-Council on 23 July 1990.[1] It will enter into force only after ratification by the last signatory Member State. Today (February 1994) ratifications of Ireland, Greece and Portugal are still missing.

This 'European Convention' will also be the touchstone of our discussion of legal sources and recognition of taxpayer's position in international tax arbitra-

1. Convention 90/436/EEC of 23 July 1990, O.J. No. L 225. A general discussion of the Convention is found in: Hinnekens, L., 'The Tax Arbitration Convention. Its significance for the EC Based Enterprise, the EC itself, and for Belgian and International Tax Law', *EC Tax Review,* 1992/2 p. 70 – 105; Terra, B., & Wattel, P., *European Tax Law,* Kluwer, 1993, 207 – 220.

tion. The Convention itself hardly uses the expression 'arbitration', 'arbitral decision', etc. (the only exception being found in the heading of Chapter II, Section III 'Mutual agreement and arbitration procedure'). But we will see that the legal nature of the 'opinion delivered by the advisory commission to the competent authorities which take the decision' boils down, in a very real sense, to a decision rendered by a more or less independent jurisdictional organ and having a (potentially and more likely effectively) binding effect on the parties to the dispute ('acte de juridiction').

Voluntary or mandatory tax arbitration is also provided for in some (pending or signed) bilateral tax treaties, specifically between Germany and Sweden, France and the United States, and between the United States and the Netherlands and Mexico. They are only mentioned marginally.

B. Integrating Legal Sources and Concurrent Jurisdictional Procedures into European Tax Arbitration Law

Disputes between a taxpayer and his taxing State or States (e.g. concerning income re-allocation in transfer pricing cases) are the subject matter of a domestic procedure, brought by that taxpayer before the competent administrative or judicial organ in accordance with the Constitution and legal system of that State or States.

Under the European Convention the same tax dispute also becomes the subject matter of an international (or even supra-national) jurisdictional procedure. It is conducted between the competent authorities of the two or more States concerned. The arbitration commission does not arbitrate between the taxpayer and the State(s).

The two procedures do not exclude each other, but compete in most Member States. This two-track system opens a new and interesting avenue for the taxpayer, who gets a second (international) string to his bow. But, like two strings to one bow, the operation of the two concurrent jurisdictional remedies should not be conflictual. How is the coordination achieved under the European Convention, and how does it impact on the taxpayer's fundamental procedural rights?

The potential problem of conflictual relationships and the need of integration and of legal ordering also exist at the arbitral level governed by different sources of law and principles of interpretation.

We submit that the following rules apply to the European Convention and to the arbitration proceedings conducted thereunder:

1. The convention is a treaty under international law, and is, as such, governed and interpreted in accordance with rules of international law.
Under the Vienna Convention on the Law of the Treaties, the wording of the

treaty, and not the investigation *ab initio* into the Contracting Parties' intentions, is the starting point. The *text* of the European Convention, as the authentic expression of the intention of the Contracting States, governs its interpretation and application.

2. When the text of the Convention is unclear, its meaning is determined from the *context*, requiring such meaning. This interpretation rule is found in Article 3 (2) of the Convention and is in accordance with international principles of interpretation of treaties (Article 31(2) of the Vienna Convention). Article 31(1) of that Convention refers also to the (European) Convention's object and purpose.

Here are two examples under the European Convention:

The arbitration principles of the Convention are defined in its Article 4. The article provides for the right of adjustment of the profit by the State of the transferring enterprise and for the obligation of the other State to make a corresponding adjustment of the profit of the receiving enterprise. The latter obligation is not expressly stated as a principle in Article 4, but follows from the purpose itself of the Convention and from its context (e.g. Article 14 - definition and method of elimination of double taxation).

The yardstick of common adjustment applied by Article 4, is the arm's length principle. As, under the rules of international arbitration and of the Statute of the International Court of Justice, competence is based solely on the text and interpretation of the Convention, we will in our further discussion, exclude any other criteria. Or is it possible that the restrictive wording of Article 4 is sloppy language, not in accordance with the intention of the drafters of the European Convention? *Quod voluit non dixit.*

3. *Earlier arbitral decisions* do not have precedential value. They are not binding on the same or other parties in other procedures under the same European Convention.

But the decisions rendered and published will inevitably generate, if not international case law then, a doctrinal body that may (and should) generally inspire later arbitral commissions for the sake of consistency and certainty in the legal system.

This consideration is formally recognized in the Technical Explanation to the arbitration clause in the Tax Treaty between Germany and the United States: 'While the decision of the arbitration board shall not have precedential effect, it is expected that such decisions ordinarily will be taken into account in subsequent competent authority cases involving the same taxpayer(s), the same issue(s) and substantially similar facts, and may also be taken into account in other cases where appropriate'.

4. The legal relationships between the European Convention and arbitrations thereunder on the one hand, and *European Community Law* on the other, is ambivalent, as is the *sui generis* legal character of the Convention.

Is the Convention part and parcel of the European Communities' legal order? Unlike a directive ex Article 100 EC Treaty, which the Commission had initially proposed as the appropriate legal instrument for tax administration, a convention ex Article 220 EC Treaty is not part of Community law proper. It has the outward signs of an ordinary international agreement, even if it was signed in a meeting within the EC-Council (a mere figure of speech).

As such it is not subject to the obligatory jurisdiction of the European Court of Justice (Article 177 EC Treaty: 'the interpretation of this treaty'). And the Member States did not enter into a Protocol extending its jurisdiction to the European arbitration Convention and its interpretation. The European Court of Justice is, of course, competent to interpret Article 220 EC-Treaty on which the Convention is based. For instance, it may examine the very basic question of the validity of the Convention, in view of the expressly subsidiary character of the application of Article 220 EC-Treaty ('so far as is necessary') and to the pre-emptive legal force of the 1976 directive proposed and still maintained by the Commission. But as there is a little chance that the Member States accept to replace the Convention by a directive or to enter into a Protocol, the European Court is not competent to review the interpretation and application of the Convention.

If a question of (in-)compatibility of their tax laws or procedures with the EC-Treaty and directives is raised, the national courts may (or must) refer it to the European Court of Justice. But it seems farfetched to base on the EC Treaty freedoms the authority of the European Court with the respect to the European Convention e.g. by virtue of the reasoning that the free movement of capital and the free right of primary and secondary establishment are restricted by unsoluable double taxation, and therefore requires the Member States to remedy it by arbitration.

Both the Ruding Committee and the EC-Commission have stressed the need for harmonization in the field of transfer pricing. If and when the tax rules for pricing adjustments would thus become harmonized by means of a directive or coordinated by some other measure, the Member States would be required to take them into account as such, also when they apply the European Convention. The national judicial authorities will then have the power (or obligation) to refer to the European Court questions of interpretation or application of such harmonization measure.

It is another question whether the arbitral commissions, set up by the competent authorities of the Member States concerned under the European Convention, would also have that right or obligation of reference to the European Court of Justice.

It would assume, firstly, that the arbitration commission pertains to a Member State. This condition should not raise a problem, where the arbitral level is binational between Member States. It raises, secondly, the question whether the commission is instituted by law. Here again there should be no problem, as the term covers international convention as well as statutory law, etc.

More tricky is the question whether an arbitrator must be interpreted to constitute a court or tribunal, within the meaning of that term in Article 177 EC Treaty. In deciding that it had no jurisdiction to give a ruling to a German arbitrator in a State aid case, the European Court had relied on the circumstance that the parties had voluntarily agreed to the arbitration of their dispute and that public authorities had not been involved (*Nordsee* v. *Reederei Mond,* Case 102/81 (1982)). Under the European Convention the affected enterprise may present its case to the competent authority, and this authority initiates the procedure 'if the complaint appears to it to be well-founded'. But we will interpret this reservation to mean that the competent authority of that Member State is bound to initiate the procedure and to resolve the dispute by arbitration in accordance with the dictate of the European Convention, if the taxpayer's complaint is not abusive or manifestly unjustified. It can therefore be argued that the arbitration procedure is compulsory for the Member States, as they are normally forced to it by the complaint of the taxpayer. At any rate, we repeat that, if the arbitration commission would not itself be entitled to refer to the European Court under Article 177, the national court would have to consider such reference.

5. While the Convention is not part of European Community Law proper, it is still very closely connected to that legal order.

We submit that the collective exercise by the Member States of their power to enter into the Convention in accordance with Article 220 EC Treaty, gives to that Convention a superior legal value. As such it prevails on contrary provisions of present and even future DTT's also dealing with the arm's length principle, and of other treaties also dealing with arbitration procedures in a general or even more special fashion.

If the Convention would ultimately not get ratified by one or more States, the other Member States could agree to limit its effective application as among themselves. But such new convention would not have the legal value of the European Convention, if and when it would have been ratified by all Member States on the basis of Article 220 EC-Treaty.

6. On 4 November 1950 the Member States of the Council of Europe signed the *Convention for the Protection of Human Rights and Fundamental Freedoms.* It secures everyone within their jurisdiction certain fundamental rights, i.e. his entitlement to a fair and public hearing within a reasonable time by an independent and impartial tribunal established by law (Article 6 § 1).

It is controversial whether those obligations and rights also apply to procedures concerning tax arbitration. National courts and the Strasbourg Commission (in cases which did not reach the Court) considered that no civil right is at stake in tax proceedings. And learned authors caution against extending the personal and material scope of the protection beyond the restricted application, that was probably envisaged by the drafters of the Convention for the Protection of Human Rights and accepted by the European Member States. Even (or especially) in a democratic society, the national courts should remain sovereign and exclusively competent to resolve such other applications and determinations. But the Strasbourg Court considered (e.g. on 17 January 1970 in the Delcourt case) that 'in a democratic society within the meaning of this Convention, the right to a fair administration of Justice holds such a prominent place that a restrictive interpretation of Article 6 (1) would not correspond to the aim and the purpose of that provision'.

The concept 'civil rights and obligation' (initial term 'suit-at-law') also applies to disputes which are public according to their form and subject and which involve a public authority in a sovereign capacity, if their outcome is of direct interest for the determination of the patrimonial rights and obligations of the victim. And the term 'charge' must be interpreted to have a substantive, not a formal, meaning.

The expression 'everyone within the jurisdiction' is sufficiently broad to apply not only to private individuals but also to enterprises in the sense of the European Convention. The Commission of Human Rights found that the individual holding a majority shareholding in a company, but also the company itself, may lodge a complaint under Article 25 of the Convention for the Protection of Human Rights, as victims of alleged violations of their rights when a company is being nationalized (*X* v. *Austria*, Appl 1706/62; *Yarrow* v. *UK* Appl 9266/81). In our case the victims are associated enterprises suffering double taxation.

Article 1 of Protocol No. 1 deals expressly with the duty of every natural or legal person to pay tax. On the basis of this provision and that of Article 14 of the Convention, the European Court of Human Rights held on 23 October 1990 in the Darby case that an ordinary tax dispute (tax discrimination of non-residents) may violate that Convention.

On 25 December 1993 the same Court of Human Rights held in the Funke case that the Convention's principles (the right of a fair process under Article 6(1) and to respect of privacy under Article 8) were violated by a condemnation for refusal to procedure the foreign bank accounts required by customs officials (manifestly also for tax purposes).

Another forum for the enforcement of those principles of the Convention of the Protection of Human Rights, is the European Court of Justice. Article F(2) of the (Maastricht) Treaty on European Union reads as follows: 'The Union shall respect fundamental rights, as guaranteed by the European Convention for the Protection of Human Rights and Fundamental Freedoms signed in Rome on

4 November 1950 and as they result from the constitutional traditions common to the Member States, as general principles of Community law'.

Even prior to the Union Treaty, the European Court of Justice had accepted to rule on the application of the same principles in ordinary tax procedures (provided the referring national body is a court or tribunal in the sense of Article 177 EC Treaty, decision of 30 March 1993 in the Corbiau case).

The question is raised in similar terms with respect to the application of Article 14 of the International Covenant on Civil and Political Rights. It was signed in New York on 15 May 1981, also by many EC Member States. It guarantees essentially the same right to a fair hearing within a reasonable time by an independent and impartial tribunal. But, unlike the European Convention, the Covenant does not provide for an objective procedure which places the decision in the hands of a third, neutral organ.

7. What is the legal significance, for tax arbitration under the European Convention, of the *Convention on the Recognition and Enforcement of Foreign Arbitral Awards* signed in New York in 1958?

Article V of that Convention deals with grounds on which foreign arbitration awards may be refused enforcement by the national authorities at the request of the party against whom it is invoked. Such grounds may be: violation of due process for lack of proper notice or inability to present case, lack of impartiality and independence of arbitrator, lack of reasons on which decision is based, excess of arbitrator's authority, irregularity in composition of arbitral tribunal, lack of arbitrability of subject matter. They do not include a review of the merits of the award (i.e., in the case of the European Convention, whether the award is in accordance with the arm's length tax principle.)

It is uncertain whether the rules of this Convention will apply to tax arbitration decisions rendered under the European Convention.

Firstly, are such awards made in the territory of another contracting State or can they be considered as non-domestic in the Member State where their recognition and enforcement are sought? The awards under the European convention are not de-nationalized but are inter-national or even supra-national. We will see that the procedural rules of the European Convention do not (completely) oust the national laws of the particular Member States concerned.

Secondly, does the New York Convention cover arbitrations dealing with 'conditions made or imposed between associated enterprises in their commercial of financial relations' in the sense of the European Convention? Also if the Member States concerned used the possibility to restrict its application to 'differences arising out of legal relationships, which are considered as commercial under the law of the State making such declaration'? Whilst this commercial reservation must be interpreted according to the law of the forum State, the definition was intended to be generally broad and, going to our case, probably sufficiently wide to encompass also disputes conducted between public authorities but relating to the tax effects of transfer pricing of commercial and financial transactions between associated enterprises.

The New York Convention does not provide for a binational, supra-national or otherwise neutral organ to proceed with an objective review of the (denial of) application of its rules. Its principles are not incorporated in European Community Law, unless they would result from the constitutional traditions common to the Member States, in the sense of Article F(2) of the Treaty on European Union. The European Court of Justice is therefore not competent to review their observance.

The relationship between the recognition rules of the New York Convention and the concurrent rules of domestic laws and of other bilateral or multilateral treaties is dealt with in Article VII of that Convention: 'The provisions of the present Convention shall not affect the validity of multilateral or bilateral agreements concerning the recognition and enforcement of arbitral awards entered into by the contracting State, nor deprive any interested party of any right he may have to avail himself of an arbitral award in the manner and to the extent allowed by the law or the treaties of the country where such award is sought to be relied upon' (mfr-provision).

8. The legal relation between the European Convention and the *DTT's among its signatory States* is described as follows.

The European Convention recognizes expressly DDT's. It deals with the relationship in its Article 15: the Convention does affect the fulfillment of wider obligations resulting from other conventions to which the contracting States, are or will become, parties. A case in point is that in which the elimination of double taxation is still open under the applicable bilateral tax treaty whereas the time limit for arbitration under the Convention expired.

But where the European Convention provides for wider obligations (e.g. arbitration and not mere duty to negotiate an agreement), it has priority on the DDT-rule in our reading a contrario of the aforementioned provision of the Convention and in our legal analysis of the Convention as a higher ranking norm.

Many expressions used in the European Convention are not defined in it, but are defined in the applicable DTT, e.g. permanent establishment, profit of an enterprise of (i.e. a resident of) a contracting State, etc; Article 3.2 of the Convention refers to their meaning under the DTT between the Member States concerned. This interpretation rule, the sameness of the texts (in particular the wording of the principles of Article 4 of the Convention, which is almost a literal rendition of Articles 7 (2) and 9 of the OECD Model), and the consideration that the arbitration procedure is the continuation and completion of the mutual agreement procedure, permit the conclusion that their interpretation is common in both international instruments.

The Commentaries and Reports on Transfer Pricing and Multinational Enterprises of the OECD Committee on Fiscal Affairs therefore constitute an equally useful source for their common interpretation.

Sometimes the texts in both instruments are not entirely the same. The difference then raises a problem of interpretation. For instance, the principles of Article 4 (1) and (2) of the Convention may be almost identical to those of Article 7 (2) and a literal rendition of Article 9 of the DTT's according to OECD Model. But Paragraphs (1), (3), (4) and (5) of Article 7 are missing in Article 4(2) of the Convention. We submit that it means that the arbitration commissions may not apply those paragraphs. International tax specialists have pointed out that the income allocation implications and directives, on the one hand, of the arm's length rule and, on the other hand, of those other paragraphs, may not be fully consistent or compatible. It will be interesting to see what the arbitration commissions will decide when they are faced with cases of fictional profit, invented under the arm's length principle but not found in the actual profit of the permanent establishment or even of the enterprise (theory of the part in application of Article 7 (1)?), or with cases of internal expenses (application of Article 7 (3)?) and formula apportionment (application of Article 7 (4)?).

A similar interpretation problem arises with respect to the legal validity of arbitration on grounds of equity or operational practicality. The OECD Commentary would seem to allow, at least subsidiarily, such principles for mutual agreements under Article 25 (1) and (2) OECD Model. Article 25 Comm. par. 26: 'Should the strict application of such rules or provisions (of the Convention) preclude any agreement, it may reasonably be held that the competent authorities, as in case of international arbitration, can, subsidiarily, have regard to considerations of equity in order to give the taxpayer satisfàction'. But the text of the arbitration Convention requires very expressly that the arbitration must be based on the (arm's length) principle of Article 4, which does not provide for such alternative criteria. Only in the first stage of the Convention procedure, conducted in the State of residence, the decision is reached with no reference to any specific principle other that the requirement that the solution must be satisfactory (Article 6 (2)). The latter elusive test may be appropriate in the mutual agreement procedure, which is a diplomatic method for settling an international dispute. It is less acceptable in a jurisdictional system of arbitration. Does it then mean that the Convention does not permit decisions rendered in the name of *ex aequo et bono*, compromise, 'splitting the difference', package deal 'horse trading', so often applied in the practice of mutual agreements and praised as Solomon's judgments?

9. Another issue is that of the significance for the arbitration under the Convention of the *mutual agreements* reached between the competent authorities of the same States under the provision of the applicable DTT which corresponds to *Article 25 of the OECD Models.* The article distinguishes mutual agreements reached under paragraphs 1 and 2 (specific case agreements) and those reached under paragraph 3 (consultative or legislative agreements).

It is unlikely that the same individual case, resolved by a mutual agreement under those paragraphs (1) and (2), would again be resolved by arbitration under the European Convention. Article 7 of that Convention defines the conditions of access to the latter procedure as follows: 'If the competent authorities fail to reach an agreement that eliminates the double taxation'. The consideration that the mutual agreement would have been based on satisfactory principles (e.g. *ad hoc* compromises) other than those governing the arbitration procedure (Article 4 of Convention) does not constitute a sufficient ground for access to the arbitration procedure for a review of that agreement.

It is more likely that the arbitral commission is set up to render an opinion with respect to an individual case of double taxation which is not resolved by the competent authorities of the two authorities, but the relevant fiscal facts of which are similar to those of another specific case that was resolved by a mutual agreement between the same authorities of the same States (or between those of other Member States). The mutual agreement relating to one case is not binding in the mutual agreement and arbitration procedure relating to another specific case.

Still another situation is that of interpretative mutual agreements reached between the competent authorities under paragraph 3 of Article 25 of the applicable DDT. They concern the interpretation and general application of that treaty. Under this paragraph the two States, committed to the good faith performance of their undertaking to eliminate double taxation, expressly mandate their competent authorities to resolve themselves such difficulties of a general nature. A conflict between such interpretative agreements and the mutual agreements and arbitration procedures under the European Convention is again not likely to arise. The scope of application of the latter procedures is limited to income-reallocations in individual transfer pricing cases, and as such does not cover interpretation and application difficulties of a general nature affecting a category of taxpayers. But the conflict and the relationship problem may arise under the wider scope of arbitration in accordance with bilateral clauses.

Are the competent authorities and the arbitral commissions in a procedure under the Convention or a DDT clause legally bound by an interpretative or specific case agreement reached by the competent authorities of the same States under Article 25 of their DTT? Under General International Law and Article 2, I(a) of the Vienna Convention on the Law of Treaties, the term treaty or agreement between States has a very broad meaning. As a rule, it requires its formal ratification in accordance with the constitutional laws of the States. But a delegation of powers to this effect is implied in the agreements in simplified forms ('accords en forme simplifiée'). We do not believe that a mutual agreement between competent authorities under Article 25 DTT or of Article 6(2) of the Convention constitutes itself treaty law, not even a treaty in simplified form. It forms an intergovernmental agreement of a purely administrative nature ('arrangement administratif'), designed to implement the administration of the only existing and authentic DTT.

The mutual agreement is therefore not legally binding on the individual States, on their courts and on the arbitral commission, which the competent authorities would set up as a jurisdictional organ. But it is a good source of inspiration for the courts and the arbitrator, as it points out to a common interpretation or application that can be accepted by both States ('Gebot der Entscheidungsharmonie').

10. The European tax arbitration Convention only deals with the elimination of double taxation of profits of associated enterprises of different Member States. It does not deal with profits made between an enterprise of a Member State and its associated enterprise, or even its own permanent establishment, in a third country. It thus offers no solution to cases unresolved by mutual agreement under a *DDT with a third country.*

But the doctrinal body created by arbitration under the European Convention may also inspire bilateral arbitral decisions, mutual agreements. APA's, etc., outside the scope of application of that Convention. Authorities of a Member State can not force the authorities of a third country to accept the opinions, which they themselves must accept under the Convention in other cases or even in the same (multi-country transfer pricing) case. But, for the sake of consistency in their legal system, they will endeavor to apply, also in their relation with third countries, the solutions which they apply in their relation with Member States. Joint initiatives of coordination between EC and OECD in this area are probably unavoidable.

11. The *Principles of General International Law* apply to the interpretation and application of the European Convention and the arbitration procedures thereunder, as they are of limited use, in the field of taxation, even aside from the problem of their enforceability.

In particular General International Law provides for no principle dealing with the elimination of international double taxation as a result of the concurrence of fiscal jurisdiction e.g. in transfer pricing cases. It constitutes no international procedure to settle overlapping fiscal jurisdiction of States and does not require them to take the jurisdictional measures necessary to eliminate it. It is simply indifferent to it.

Absolute equity has occasionally been recognized and applied as a principle of General International Law in certain (non-fiscal) international arbitration awards, by the Permanent Court of International Justice and by the International Court of Justice (e.g. in the North Sea Continental Shelf Cases, Rec. CIJ 1969, 43). But we concluded that such principles are probably excluded from the Convention and the arbitrations thereunder, on grounds of fiscal indefiniteness and of the restrictive definition of its governing principles in Article 4. But the tax arbitration clauses of some bilateral treaties expressly refer to it: 'giving due consideration to the principles of international law' and 'generally accepted principles of equity' (points 3 and 5 of the Technical Explanation, Article 25 of tax treaty between Germany and US).

The Vienna Convention of the Law of Treaties and other international interpretation principles and customary law not codified by that Convention apply also to the interpretation and application of the European Convention. But we concluded that rules as '*lex posterior derogat legi priori*' and '*lex specialis derogat legi generali*' can probably not apply to the relation between ordinary tax treaties and the European Convention ('*lex superior derogat legi inferiori*').

Last but not least: what is the legal relationship between the principles and procedures of the European Convention and those of the *domestic laws of the States concerned?*

The 'international sauce', served with the European Convention, is based on a principle of General International Law: a treaty between States, and arbitral commissions set up under it to adjudicate disagreements between those States, are governed exclusively by the rules of international law. It establishes the formal autonomy of the international rule and remedy, and the exclusion of the national rule as such, even if the undertakings of the contracting States and the decision of their arbitration commission effectively deal with the other dispute between the taxing States and the taxpayer under the national tax laws and procedures.

But this 'international sauce' does not imply that international arbitration is completely detached from the ambit and normative influence of the national law. This conclusion is clear where the application of the latter is recognized and regulated expressly in the Convention itself.

Article 15 provides that nothing in the Convention shall affect the fulfillment of wider obligations resulting from domestic law. The Convention thus sets only minimum standards and recognizes additional national remedies outside its scope.

The Convention does not expressly deal with conflict situations in which domestic law imposes less of an obligation (to eliminate double taxation in transfer pricing cases). But if the application of the Convention rule would not already be implied in the aforementioned article and the aim and object of Convention itself, it follows form the other public international principle of the supremacy of the treaty rule in norm hierarchy of the States concerned. In coming to this conclusion, we have attributed a self-executing effect to the arbitration undertaking under the Convention, in view of its clear obligation to eliminate double taxation and its sufficient regulation of the legal framework.

Other Convention articles are permissive, and allow the competent authorities of the States concerned to depart from them or to defer their application. For example, if the domestic law does not permit the national authorities to derogate from the decisions of their own judicial bodies, their obligation to set up an arbitral commission applies only if the enterprise lets expire the time limit for domestic appeals or withdraws such appeals (Article 7(3)). And the national authorities may refuse to initiate, or may stay, the proceedings where judicial or administrative proceedings are initiated with a view to a ruling that the actions are liable to a serious penalty (Article 8).

Article 10 of the Convention provides that the obligations called for by that article (to provide information and documentation) can not be at variance with the domestic law or administrative practice.

The interpretation rule of Article 3(2) of the European Convention refers for the meaning of its undefined terms to their meaning in the double taxation agreements between the States concerned, which in turn refer to the *lex fori* (Article 3(2) OECD Model).

An express and general reference to domestic tax laws is found in some bilateral arbitration clauses or in their Technical Explanation e.g. to the treaty between Germany and the United States: 'The arbitration board shall decide each specific case on the basis of the Convention giving due consideration to the domestic laws of the Contracting States'.

No such general reference is found in the text of the Convention. But even in the absence of such express provision the domestic laws of the States concerned find a subsidiary and amplifying application. The Convention is not always articulate in the the elaboration of the terms of its practical implementation. Examples are found in each stage of the international procedure, but especially in that of the initiation and that of the execution: how will the enterprise validly lodge its complaint? What interest, if any, is due on late tax payments or accruable on tax refunds? How will the arbitration award be technically executed *vis-à-vis* the States? The formal autonomy of the Convention rule hardly hides its dependence on the domestic 'contentieux fiscal'.

The acceptance of this amplifying effect of domestic law on DTT's is found in Article 25 Comm. par. 5 of the Report of the EOCD Committee 1977: 'Since the Article merely lays down general rules concerning the mutual agreement procedure; the comments now following are intended to clarify the purpose of such rules, and also to amplify them, if necessary, by referring, in particular, to the rules followed at the internal level in the conduct of the procedures which exist in most OECD Member countries for dealing with disputed claims regarding taxes.' The conceptual justification and practical necessity of integrating domestic procedural rules *per analogia* = *m* into the international procedure, was supposedly even greater for the drafters of the European Convention in view of its guaranteed outcome, irrespective of the many gaps created by their regulation in sufficient detail. The legal protection and certainty of the taxpayer require such unity of legal system.

National law regulations and case law are, by their unilateral nature and divergence, admittedly not an ideal source of interpretation of multilateral (European Convention) or bilateral treaty clauses. But the 'bad habit' of national administrations and courts to interpret bilateral tax treaties unilaterally, much in the same manner as they interpret their domestic tax statute, is in practice less of a risk for an arbitration commission, which is a more or less neutral and impartial jurisdictional body composed of representatives of both States concerned and of independents. As the Convention is concluded between EC Member States, it offers also better practical prospects and possibilities for the domestic amplification of its international rule and adjudication process (central collection, notification, translation of documentation concerning relevant statutory provisions, administrative regulations and practice, rulings and judicial decisions)

C. Recognizing the Legal Position of the Enterprise in International (European) Tax Arbitration

Having described the legal sources of international tax arbitration specifically under the European Convention, we now examine their contribution of the definition of the legal position of the enterprise in the arbitration procedures thereunder.

The need for recognition of the enterprise and for a definition of its position, is much greater in international tax arbitration than in the mutual agreements procedure. Both procedures are international remedies designed to resolve a double taxation problem for the enterprise. In the latter procedure the tax administrations of the two States concerned negotiate to this effect a mutual agreement, which is not binding on their national courts. The courts have, in principle, their hands free to settle the same tax dispute. The arbitration procedure changes the legal nature of the mechanism from diplomatic into jurisdictional: a third, neutral and even supranational body is instituted, which renders a decision which is binding on the States concerned, their tax administrations and their courts. It thus becomes indirectly but effectively also binding on the enterprise.

Its interest in the procedure is recognized and protected by making it a (quasi-, semi-, or pseudo-) party to the arbitration, which thus becomes almost a tri-party procedure. The reservation ('quasi', 'almost') reflects the fact that the arbitration procedure, even when it duly recognizes the legitimate interest of the taxpayer by giving him a more active participation and procedural rights in it, is still conducted solely between the competent authorities of the States concerned, and deals with the tax dispute as between those States.

The taxpayer's position under the European Convention differs from the (more or less far-reaching) recognition of his position in other (bilateral) tax arbitration procedures, but is generally described by his right to procedural fairness. This concept is not defined in abstracto, as it must take into account the context and course of the individual arbitration proceedings.

The following enumeration of rights does not define in any exhaustive manner the taxpayer's legal position in the arbitration procedures under the European Convention.

1. Right of Initiative

Article 6(2) of the European Convention provides that the taxpayer has the right to present his case to the competent authority of the State of his residence or of his permanent establishment.

The competent authority is responsible for initiating the procedure, but may in principle not refuse to do so. It must normally set in motion the procedure which is mandatory (referral is voluntary in many bilateral arbitration clauses.)

2. Refusal of Initiation by Competent Authority must not constitute an Abuse

This legal right of initiative of the taxpayer risks to be eroded, if he has no legal claim ('Rechtsanspruch') to force his competent authority to set the procedure in motion. Article 6(2) of the Convention provides that the competent authority shall resort to the mutual agreement procedure, if (and only if) 'the complaint appears to it to be well-founded'.

On the basis of this language, it can be argued that the obligation of the national authority under this provision is not sufficiently precise and unconditional to be deemed self executing and to provide the taxpayer an autonomous basis to seek enforcement of his right by bringing his case directly to the national court if the authority would fail to initiate the mutual agreement procedure. It can also be argued that the obligation found in Article 9(2) OECD Model 1977 ('When the contracting State includes in the profits . . . profits on which the enterprise of the other contracting State has been charged to tax . . . than that other State shall make an appropriate adjustment') does not provide for any right of initiative to the taxpayer. But this is not the view of the Fiscal Committee which finds that such taxation is not in accordance with the provisions of the Convention so that again Article 25(1) and (2) confers that right of initiative to the complainant.

We never interpreted the language in Article 25 §2 of the OECD Model as a *conditio potestativa*. The absolute discretion on the part of the competent authority would frustrate the useful effect of the agreement, and violate the performance in good faith by that authority of its international undertaking. The paragraph becomes even less discretionary where, as in the European Convention, it is applied to a mutual agreement procedure which conditions the access to the mandatory arbitration, in which the States formally undertake to settle their dispute and to eliminate the double taxation in a sufficiently defined legal framework.

The competent authority of the State concerned may also not refuse to take the case because it would fall outside the scope of the Convention pursuant to an interpretation that would be clearly unreasonable and abusive on its part. Such unjustified refusal would again violate the State's obligation to perform the Convention in good faith.

We saw that our interpretation is also important because of its consequences for the application of the procedural fairness guarantees under other international treaties if it means that the procedure is compulsory for the States as required for the application of such other treaties.

3. Obligations of Competent Authorities not Absolute

The obligations of the competent authorities (to initiate the procedure upon presentation by the enterprise of its case, to set up an arbitration commission, to provide information to it, and to carry out the administrative measures requested by it, etc.) are not absolute. They are subject to the exception of (absence of) abuse on the part of the enterprise lodging the complaint, of its manifestly ill-founded merits, of liability to a serious penalty in connection with its tax evading practices, of disclosures (not-being) contrary to public policy and of administrative measures (not-being) at variance with domestic laws and administrative practice.

These exceptions are found in the European Convention. But here again the competent authorities shall, in accordance with international principles of good faith performance of their arbitration obligations, refrain from their unreasonable or abusive application. For instance, they may not refuse arbitration by lodging a criminal or administrative complaint against the enterprise engaging in the manipulative transfer pricing practice, for the sole purpose of unjustifiedly applying the escape hatch set out in the Convention for serious penalty cases.

Bilateral arbitration clauses provide that the competent authorities may agree to invoke arbitration only after fully exhausting other available remedies, or if the taxpayer consents to be bound by the arbitration decision, if he agrees to bear that contracting State's share of the costs as a prerequisite for arbitration (Protocol to treaty between Germany and the United States).

4. Right to require Discontinuation of Procedure

The question is raised whether the Contracting States should be able to continue the arbitration procedure against the will of the taxpayer. Shouldn't he have the right to require the competent authorities to stop the procedure, after setting it in motion by lodging his complaint?

The Convention does not provide for such right. This is consistent with the view that only the States are party proper to it. But we would argue for a more active involvement of the taxpayer also with respect to this decision.

5. Right to a Reasonable Time Framework

International treaties and principles prescribe the right to a hearing within a reasonable time. The time framework should be adequate, i.e. sufficiently long for presenting the case and sufficiently short for coming to a decision.

The succesive periods set out in the European Convention are adequate: three years for presenting the case, two years for establishing the arbitration commission (which time limit may be extended, but only with the taxpayer's consent), six months for the commission to deliver its opinion, another six months for the competent authorities to deviate from it.

6. Right of Access to Information, e.g. concerning Other Arbitral Decisions

The international treaties and principle concerning the subject's right to transparency in the exercise of public authority, and possibly also that of equal arms, imply the taxpayer's right of access to information concerning the commission's sources to the extent they play a rôle in the commission's opinion.

It raises the problem of how to combine his legitimate interest in this disclosure of earlier arbitral decisions with the equally legitimate interest in the protection of taxpayer's business secrets. It is resolved in Article 12 of the Convention by the requirement of taxpayer's consent to the publication.

7. Right to provide Information and Documentation

In accordance with the fair hearing principle, Article 10 (1) of the Convention provides that the enterprises concerned may provide any information, evidence or documents (economist's opinions, etc.), which seem to them likely to be of use to the commission.

8. Right to Appear or to be Present or Represented

This right is prescribed by the international principle of fair hearing, which requires the opportunity for all affected parties (or semi-parties) to be present or represented when the case is being reviewed.

It is expressly provided for in Article 10 (2) of the European Convention.

9. Right to Refuse to Provide Certain Information Requested by the Arbitral Commission

The taxpayer's right of refusal applies whenever the information and documentation are not obtainable under domestic law or administrative practice, or if they disclose his trade or business secrets.

The right is not expressly provided for in the Convention. But it is implied in its providing this same right to the competent authorities, and in the consideration that the drafters did not intend and that the aim and purpose of the Convention could not be to curtail the taxpayer's right to arbitration and elimination of his double taxation by his fear of being obliged to disclose his trade secrets.

May the enterprise refuse to supply information and documentation requested by the commission on the ground of the international principle of right to refuse self-incriminating statements or documents because of the risk that the revenue representatives may use them. But an inquiry of the arbitration commission is not a charge against the taxpayer, who has the protection of the secrecy obligation of its members.

One wonders whether, in the balancing of the interest of the revenue authorities and that of the enterprise in protecting its trade secrets, the latter interest should not receive greater weight in the arbitration procedure under the Convention, and the former interest greater weight in the system of exchange of information among the competent authorities. Whereas the object of arbitration is the elimination of double taxation, that of the obligation of exchange is to secure the application of domestic tax laws. But the wording of the trade secrecy protection reservation is in essence the same. A different interpretation of the right and obligation respectively under the European arbitration Convention and the under EC Directive on Mutual Assistance (77/799/EEC) should be avoided.

10. Opportunity to Refuse the Arguments and Evidence of the Revenue Authorities

The procedure should be contradictory, also as far as the taxpayer is concerned.

Whilst he has the guarantee that, whatever decision is reached, it must eliminate double taxation, he has a further interest in the terms of the solution i.e. in the allocation of his income to the one or to the other State. He should therefore be given the opportunity to hear, improve or refute the presentations by the respective competent authorities.

This right is not expressly provided for in the Convention, but is probably implied in the right of the enterprise to appear before the commission at its request, and to supply the information which he deems useful for his case. At any rate it is in accordance with the principles of fair hearing and equality of arms.

11. Right to Independent and Impartial Jurisdiction

The independence and impartiality of the arbitration commissions are important as a safeguard and protection for the taxpayer, but also for their jurisdictional characterization as courts or tribunals which conditions the access to several international treaties.

The system of arbitration under the European Convention and in particular its rules concerning composition and qualification requirements, is somewhat hybrid.

The system firstly raises a problem of numbers. The European Convention calls for an equal number of representatives on the part of the authorities of both States concerned, and for an even number (which becomes uneven because of the Chairman) of independents. The balance is thus established as between the competent authorities of the two States concerned, but not as between the aggregate number of all representatives of the revenue authorities and that of independent persons. In this system the independent vote prevails in the case of a tie between the votes of the two competent authorities, or if the number (e.g. 4 + 1 = 5) of independents would exceed that (e.g. 2 + 2 = 4) of all revenue representatives. In other compositions it will not prevail on the combined vote of the revenue representatives.

In arbitration proceedings the third arbitrator is the center of gravity. The *prima facie* imbalance in favor of the revenue authorities' vote must be qualified by the consideration that the adversary parties in the arbitration are the authorities of the two States concerned. On that arbitral level the equal voting is guaranteed. The taxpayer is not indifferent to the outcome of their vote but has the protection, apart from the guarantee of the elimination of double taxation of his income, of the independent vote in case of a tie between the votes of the competent authorities.

The system of the Convention raises a second problem. Even the independent persons are nominations by the revenue authorities. But they must be persons of standing, and the chairman should have the qualifications required for the appointment to the highest judicial offices in his country or be a jurisconsult of recognized competence. These requirements offer protection in the fields of impartiality and legal skills. They offer little guarantee of competence in the specific area of the case at hand. The determination of arm's length pricing in integrated multinational concerns requires economic and other specialized expertise. Any guarantees as to the commission's familiarity with the taxpayer's line of business is missing in the Convention, which provides for the nomination, once and for all, of five independent persons by each contracting State.

Thirdly, unlike the revenue authorities the enterprise has no right of eviction of a nominee (on the grounds of lack of impartiality, conflict of interest, etc.). The risk highlights the need of post-award controls.

12. Secrecy Obligation for Commission Members

The secrecy obligation is set forth in Article 9 (6) of the Convention

The obligation was deemed sufficiently important for the drafters of the Convention to require Member States to adopt measures to penalize any breach of this obligation and to involve the Commission of the European Communities in those measures.

The commission members representing the competent authorities may also not disclose matters which they learn in the proceedings to their colleagues in the tax administration, if it is likely that they may become involved in (parallel or subsequent) administration or criminal proceedings against the same taxpayer in the same case. The national statute that would require such disclosures from the commission's representatives in their capacity of revenue agents, can not be applied under the Convention.

13. Right to Motivation by the Arbitral Commission

The obligation of motivation is not expressly called for by the European Convention.

Article 11(1) only provides that the advisory commission must base its opinion on Article 4. We doubt that a self-serving statement to the effect that the opinion is delivered and the decision rendered in accordance with the principles of Article 4, is adequate.

The principle of express motivation is becoming widely accepted in international public law and constitutional traditions and is being applied also to the resolution of tax disputes. It is implied in the effective application of the fair trial and transparency principles. Where these international principles would not be self-executing, they are becoming increasingly enshrined in national statutes. The adoption of such national statutes in both Member States concerned has an amplifying effect with respect to this obligation under the European Convention.

14. Fair Allocation of Costs of Procedure

The Convention provides for an equal sharing of the commission's costs by the two Contracting States (Article 11(3)). The taxpayer bears his own costs. As the latter costs are under his control, there is little risk that they become excessive to the point of impairing his right of access to the procedure.

In this system international principles of procedural fairness are respected.

15. Fair Solution of Interest Issue

The European Convention provides for no rules on the subject matter of interest payable on late tax payments or accruable on tax refunds.

It must be resolved in accordance with the domestic laws of the States concerned. Those domestic rules are incongruous. But the Convention does not purport to harmonize them. Neither does European Community Law.

16. Right of Recourse to Remedies Available under Domestic Law

Under the European Convention the taxpayer has the right, not the obligation, to go for the international rather than for the domestic procedure. In most countries he also does not, by bringing his case to the competent authorities under the international procedure, lose his right of initiating the national procedure. In the procedure before the national court, the taxpayer is a party proper, and is entitled to the procedural protection relating to such legal capacity in accordance with national and international principles.

17. No Right to Appeal from Arbitration Decision

The international arbitration decision under the European Convention is not reviewable as to its merits by a domestic court. The finality of the arbitration does not follow from the text of the Convention. It is in accordance with its level of international (supranational) jurisdiction.

The mutual agreement proper has no such jurisdictional but only administrative force and effect. It does not bind the parties and does not limit the domestic jurisdictional remedies available to the taxpayer.

18. Right to Post-award Controls

Article 13 of the Convention provides that the finality of the decisions taken by the Contracting States shall not prevent recourse to the international procedures. If we read this provision to mean that an earlier final decision of the national court does not prevent taxpayer's right to appeal from it under the international procedure, such interpretation would be an unnecessary reminder of the provision of Article 6(1) (that the international procedure is available irrespective of the remedies provided by the domestic law of the Contracting States). It would also not explain the sequence of the articles in the Convention (after the article dealing with the decision of the competent authorities as parties to the international procedure).

Alternatively the provision of Article 13 may be interpreted to refer to the (non-)finality of the arbitral award and the right of the enterprise to bring its case again to its competent authority for (re-) hearing under the international procedure of the Convention. It would thus refer to a review of the merits (decision not in accordance with the arm's length (principle). It is uncertain under that principle, that the re-hearing can be based on procedural defects of the arbitral decision. Even if it would, the requirement that the three year timelimit for lodging complaints under the Convention must still be open, may in practice be difficult to fulfill. Article 13 would thus offer inadequate protection to the taxpayer.

His right to such protection raises the issue of the availability, also for tax arbitrations under the European Convention, of the post-award controls provided for in the New York Convention.

The taxpayer should have the right to such control mechanisms when the recognition and enforcement is sought in his forum State or arbitral awards which show such serious defects as irregularity in the composition of the arbitral commission, violation of due process, excess of arbitrator's authority, etc.

D. Conclusion

Multinational enterprise suffers from the double taxation of its profits arising from its increasingly integrated business in today's regional (European) and global markets. The arm's length price functions as the common yardstick for cross border pricing between its units. But the yardstick is elusive. Multinational enterprise is looking for effective international procedures to prevent (by APA's) or to resolve (by arbitration) double taxation in transfer pricing disputes that do not get otherwise resolved, unilaterally or by mutual agreement.

International tax arbitration is an innovating jurisdictional method. It is provided for in the European Convention and in the bilateral double taxation treaties between some States. It is hoped that its present scope of application will be extended to other (OECD-)countries, to other cases of international double taxation (e.g. resulting from different application of permanent establishment and other treaty terms), and to curing other international tax evils (e.g. discriminatory and extraterritorial taxation).

International tax arbitration also raises new legal issues. We highlighted the need to better integrate the rules of different sources of law in its legal systems, and to better recognize and define the legal position of the taxpayer in it.

Discussing international tax arbitration and its legal principles is still a somewhat arcane and experimental exercise in tax doctrine. It is also a daunting and unexplored path for the States, which traditionally pride themselves of their sovereign executive tax jurisdiction. But multinational enterprise can not wait breaking new grounds.

CONTROL MECHANISMS IN INTERNATIONAL TAX ARBITRATION

Professor William W. Park

Introduction

To reduce international tax evasion, fiscal authorities sometimes adjust the taxable profits earned by multinational enterprises in connection with intra-group sales, services or loans. Amounts charged by one member of a corporate family to another might be increased or reduced, depending on the factual configuration of the case, to reflect the fair market values of comparable transactions concluded on an 'arm's length' basis with unrelated parties.

When income is allocated to one member of a corporate group in order to 'correct' its taxable profits, correlative adjustments should normally be made to the income of the other party or parties to the relevant intra-group transactions. For example, the United States Internal Revenue Services might allocate income to an American parent corporation to reflect what it considers the proper royalty due under a patent license to a Ruritanian subsidiary. In turn, the Ruritanian subsidiary will want to deduct of the larger royalty figure in calculating its own taxable profits.

In an international context, however, symmetrical income adjustments do not always happen automatically. Inconsistent transfer pricing calculations can mean inter-company mismatching of items of income and deduction. Economic double taxation will result when some portion of group profits are taxed in the hands of more than one related party. For example, in the patent license illustration of the preceding paragraph, Ruritanian tax authorities might have a different view from the Internal Revenue Service of the value of the patent, and thus not allow the subsidiary to deduct the increased amounts taken into income by the American parent.

Arbitration pursuant to international income tax treaties presents one way to reduce such inconsistent cross-border income allocations among related taxpayers. Other tax questions appropriate for submission to arbitration include the source of income, attribution of income and expenses to a permanent establishment, and the the tax status of an individual taxpayer.[1]

1. *See* David R. Tillinghast, 'The Choice of Issues to be Submitted to Arbitration Under Income Tax Conventions', in *Essays on International Taxation In Honor of Sidney I. Roberts* 349 (H. Alpert and K. van Raad eds., 1993); Gustaf Lindencrona and Nils Mattsson, *Arbitration in Taxation* →

Arbitration of international tax controversies represents the convergence of two distinct trends in dispute resolution: (i) at attempt to reduce the time and expense of court litigation, and (ii) the pursuit of adjudicatory neutrality. The first concern has driven much of the recent Alternative Dispute Resolution (ADR) movement within the United States, where arbitration has been seen as a way to reduce the cost and delay of litigation. On the other hand, the principal *raison d'être* of international commercial arbitration has long been the enhancement of political and procedural neutrality, rather than any economy of time or money. When a company in Boston concludes a joint venture with an Algerian state agency, neither party wants to end up litigating in the other side's home court.

Considerations of efficiency and neutrality come together in arbitration of tax disputes pursuant to income tax treaties.[2] Arbitrators chosen from third countries are less likely to arouse fears of bias and political influence than judges from the respective taxing jurisdictions. And arbitration by industry experts may be more cost-effective and practical than court litigation in resolving the economically complex issues implicated by transfer pricing.

Human nature being what it is, balanced standards and procedures for the review of arbitral awards are critical to the success of international tax arbitration. Experience in commercial arbitration gives ample evidence that even the most carefully selected arbitrators are not immune to the temptations of overreaching and fraud. After the award is rendered it sometimes comes to light that an arbitrator had undisclosed links to one of the parties or disregarded the terms of the arbitral mission. While the goal of adjudicatory finality requires a bar to re-litigation of questions already decided by an arbitral tribunal, the interests of the parties will be ill served by a condition arbitral anarchy lacking controls that promote respect for the arbitrators' mission and the basic norms of procedural fairness.

I. The Contours of Nullity

In commercial arbitration, lawyers have argued for decades about how to deal with procedural defects such as arbitrator bias, corruption or excess of

→ (1981); American Law Institute, *International Aspects of United States Income Taxation* II (H. Ault, D. Tillinghast and S. Shay, Reporters, 1992) at pages 109 – 111; Lotfi Maktouf, 'Resolving International Tax Disputes Through Arbitration', 4 *Arbitration International* (No. 1) 32 (1988); Jean-Pierre Le Gall, 'Fiscalité et Arbitrage', 1994 *Revue de l'Arbitrage 3.*

2. On interpretation of tax treaties in general, *see* Hugh J. Ault, 'The Role of the OECD Commentaries in the Interpretation of Tax Treaties', in *Essays on International Taxation In Honor of Sidney I. Roberts* 61 (H. Alpert and K. van Raad eds., 1993).

authority.[3] While arbitral awards generally should be conclusive on the substantive merits of a dispute, they will not usually be treated as binding if the arbitrator exceeded the scope of jurisdiction conferred by the parties. Arbitrators have the right to be wrong, but not to re-write the parties' contract. No arbitral regime has ever provided for enforcement of an award rendered in manifest disregard of the party-imposed limits on the arbitrators' authority.[4]

Most arbitration treaties and statutes set forth control mechanisms that enumerate those defects in procedural fairness which will justify non-recognition of an arbitrator's findings. Some treaties and most statutes also establish procedures by which awards can be explicitly annulled.

Similar control issues are bound to arise in tax arbitration, particularly in connection with complex questions of inter-company transfer pricing.[5] Imagine that arbitrators have been asked to decide dispute concerning royalties paid by a subsidiary to a parent. The parent country tax authorities might determine that the licensor should realize income of 8%, while the subsidiary country authorities, concerned about exaggerated deductions, think that a 3% rate is more reasonable. In determining the royalty rate, the arbitrators might (intentionally or by inadvertence) take into account transactions with a related third company outside the scope of the arbitral agreement. Or, the arbitrators might express an opinion about arm's length interest rates on inter-company loans. In such cases, courts might disregard the award as reaching beyond the arbitrators' jurisdiction. An agreement to be bound to an arbitral decision does not constitute acceptance of an award rendered in excess of the arbitrator's scope of authority.

Typically the question of control would arise when the revenue authorities rely on the award in an action for collection of the tax, or the taxpayer relies on the award in an action for a refund. In contrast to commercial arbitration, courts would not enforce a tax award by attaching assets of the losing party

3. *See* generally, W. Michael Reisman, *Systems of Control in International Arbitration* (1992); William W. Park, 'National Law and Commercial Justice: Safeguarding Procedural Integrity in International Arbitration', 63 *Tulane Law Review* 647 (1989); W. Laurence Craig, William W. Park and Jan A.S. Paulsson, *International Chamber of Commerce Arbitration* (2d ed. 1990), Chapter 28.
4. Even the Belgian and Swiss regimes do not require courts to enforce defective awards. Article 1717 of the Belgian *Code judiciaire* and Article 192 of the Swiss *LDIP* prevent only the annulment of an award where rendered.
5. Concerning 'appropriate adjustments' to taxation of 'associated enterprises', *see* e.g. Article 9, US-German Income Tax Treaty. On the different approaches to transfer pricing, *see* Sven-Olaf Lodin, 'Is the American Approach Fair?' in *Essays on International Taxation In Honor of Sidney I. Roberts* 265 (H. Alpert and K. van Raad eds., 1993); Richard Hammer, 'Will the Arm's Length Standard Stand the Test of Time?' *id.* at 201. On recent developments in the American approach to transfer pricing, *see* generally Raymond Wacker, Allan Karnes and Randall Hahn, 'The Comparable Profits Method Under the Temporary Section 482 Regulations: A Radical Attempt to Introduce an Objective Standard for International Transfer-Pricing Activities', 11 *International Tax & Business Lawyer* 26 (1993).

(one of the two governments), but rather would be called upon to recognize the award in a collateral proceeding involving the taxpayer.

For example, assume that arbitrators find that Company X in the United States should have earned $36 million of income from transactions with its German subsidiary. In an American court proceeding for collection of the tax, either the Internal Revenue Service or Company X might present the award as the basis for calculation of Company X's tax liability. The American court would be asked to recognize the arbitrators' finding, but not to enforce the award against German tax authorities that might take an inconsistent position with respect to the transfer pricing.

This difference between recognition and enforcement of awards is important in light of the sovereign immunity that would normally protect the respective governments that are parties to tax treaty arbitration. Generally the assets of a foreign sovereign are immune from execution except when used in a commercial activity or when the sovereign has waived its immunity.[6]

At present tax treaties are silent on grounds for non- recognition of awards, usually doing no more than to affirm that tax awards will be binding. For example, the Letter of Undertanding implementing the arbitration provisions in new German-American income tax treaty provides only that 'the decision of the arbitration board in a particular case shall be binding on both Contracting States and the taxpayer with respect to that case'.[7] The European Community Convention on Double Taxation[8] provides that the competent authorities of Member States 'shall be obliged to act in accordance with' the arbitral opinion unless they take a decision that deviates from the award within six months from the date of the award.[9] This silence about the basis on which an award might be refused recognition leaves arbitrators with little guidance about vital questions of arbitral procedures (such as whether an award must state rea-

6. *See* discussion of sovereign immunity in William W. Park, 'L'Arbitrage et le recouvrement des prêts consentis à des débiteurs étrangers', 37 *McGill Law Journal* 375 (1992) at 388 – 392 and 398 – 399.

7. Letter of Understanding, United States-German Income Tax Treaty, Vernon Walters, US Ambassador to Germany, signed on 29 August 1989. *See* Paragraph 5, concerning Treaty Article 25(5). *See* also Treasury Department Technical Explanation of the Treaty, which repeats verbatim the language of Ambassador Walters. The Letter of Understanding provides that the arbitral tribunal shall consist of at least three members, with each competent authority appointing the same number, and the party-appointed members appointing the remaining arbitrators.

8. European Community Convention on the Elimination of Double Taxation in Connection with the Adjustment of Profits of Associated Enterprises. *See* Convention No. 90/435, 23 July 1990, published in 33 *Official Journal of the European Communities* (No. L 225) 10 (20 August 1990). *See* generally discussion in Luc Hinnekens, 'The Arbitration Convention: Its Significance for the EC Based Enterprise, The EC Itself and for Belgian and International Tax Law', *EC Tax Review*, 1992 No. 2, at 70. *See also* Jean-Marie Henckaerts, 'The EC Arbitration Convention for Transfer Pricing Disputes', 10 *Journal of International Arbitration* (No 3), page 111 (1993).

9. *See* Convention Article 12(1), which speaks of 'advisory commission' opinions rather than awards.

sons), and invites national courts to develop inconsistent standards for recognition of awards.

Control mechanisms in arbitration generally operate *after* the award has been rendered, when a losing party asserts that the award exceeds the arbitrators' authority or was procured by fraud or other improper means. However, questions of control can also arise *before* the arbitration begins, if tax authorities raise subject matter objections analogous to the 'arbitrability' limits known in commercial arbitration.[10] The Letter of Understanding accompanying the German-American Income Tax Treaty restricts the issues that may be submitted to arbitration by stating that 'the competent authorities will not generally accede to arbitration with respect to matters concerning the tax policy or domestic tax law of either Contracting State'.[11] A literal interpretation of this restriction may leave little to the jurisdiction to the arbitrators, other than questions that can be formulated exclusively in terms of a treaty issue.[12]

Efforts to design post-award control mechanisms for international tax arbitration will raise three basic questions: (1) what grounds should justify non-recognition of an award, (2) what (if any) bi-national procedures should be available for explicit annulment or setting aside of an award, and (3) what existing multilateral arbitration treaties already cover tax arbitration?

A. Grounds for Non-recognition

Most commercial arbitration treaties provide for the non-recognition of awards based on arbitrator bias, excess of authority or denial of one party's ability to present its case. In addition, all but two of the major arbitral centers provide non-waivable annulment procedures for defects in procedural fairness.

10. In commercial arbitration, analogous 'arbitrability' limitations have now largely been eroded, but were problematic at a time not so long ago when courts refused to order arbitration of some subject matters implicating 'public law' questions such as antitrust and securities regulations. *See* William W. Park, 'Private Adjudicators and the Public Interest: The Expanding Scope of International Arbitration', 12 *Brooklyn Journal of International Law* 629 (1986); William W. Park, W. Lawrence Craig and Jan Paulsson, *International Chamber of Commerce Arbitration* (Second Edition, 1990), Ch. 33; Rodriguez de Quijas v. Shearson/American Express, 490 US 477 (1989).
11. Clause 1 of the Letter of Understanding of Ambassador Walters, *supra*, concerning Article 25 of the US-German Income Tax Treaty. *See* generally David R. Tillinghast, 'The Choice of Issues to Be Submitted to Arbitration Under Income Tax Conventions', in *Essays on International Taxation In Honor of Sidney I. Roberts* 349 (H. Alpert and K. van Raad eds., 1993). Tillinghast notes that 'the International Revenue Service may very well take the position that the propriety of applying [transfer pricing rules based on the 'commensurate with income' standard or the 'comparable profit method'] to determine transfer prices cannot be the subject of arbitration because these are matters concerning the tax policy or domestic tax law of the United States'. *Id.* at 355.
12. For example, transfer pricing questions might be couched in terms of Article 9 of the US-German treaty concerning 'Associated Enterprises'.

Even these two exceptions, however, permit escape from judicial review only in arbitrations exclusively between non-residents.[13]

Although terminology may differ from system to system, grounds for non-recognition and/or annulment are based on many common concepts related to the procedural integrity of the arbitration, as enumerated in the selected treaty and statutory provisions set forth in the Appendix. For example, the notion of 'excess of authority' is sometimes characterized as a 'decision on matters beyond the scope of the submission to arbitration'.[14] Occasionally arbitral regimes will speak of nullity for improper constitution of the arbitral tribunal,[15] arbitrator conflict of interest or misconduct.[16]

Some arbitral systems permit non-recognition of an award that violates the forum's 'public policy',[17] or require that the award state the reasons on which the decision is based.[18] Both of these grounds for non-recognition are questionable as applied to tax arbitration.

Denial of recognition to awards on the basis that they violate a nation's public policy (*ordre public*) could open the door to excessive judicial meddling in the arbitral process. Fiscal matters by their nature usually implicate national public policy. While most lawyers can understand the reluctance of a court to enforce an award that violates its basic notions of justice and morality, a term as vague and malleable as public policy risks serving as a fig leaf to hide a judge's personal ideas of how the case should have been decided on the merits.[19]

Requiring an arbitrator to state reasons is equally problematic in fiscal arbitration. On the one hand, reasons enhance rigor in the arbitral process by making sloppy decision-making more embarrassing and permitting a court to determine whether arbitrators stayed within the limits of their authority. On the other hand, reasons contained in an award often provide the unhappy loser with ammunition for a challenge to the award and thus decrease its finality.[20]

13. In Belgium, courts are barred from hearing a request for annulment only if at least one party has a presence in Belgium. Belgian *Code judiciaire* Article 1717. In Switzerland the exclusion of the right to challenge an award must be made by an explicit agreement (*déclaration explicite*) between parties that have neither domicile, habitual residence or place of business in Switzerland. Swiss *LDIP* Article 192.
14. New York Arbitration Convention, Article V(1)(c).
15. *Id.*, Article V(1)(d).
16. Article 1904 (13), North American Free Trade Agreement, discussed *infra*.
17. *See* e.g., Swiss LDIP Article 190(2)(e); New York Convention Article V(2)(b).
18. *See* the rules of the World Bank's International Centre for the Settlement of Investment Disputes (ICSID), discussed *infra*.
19. Similar concerns have been expressed about application of the so-called 'new international law merchant', or *lex mercatoria*. *See* William W. Park, 'The Development of a Modern Lex Mercatoria', in *Lex Mercatoria and Arbitration* 109 (T. Carbonneau, ed., 1990).
20. If the arbitrator' decision was based on Regulation X, the loser might argue that the arbitral mission was limited to deciding on the basis of Regulation Y or Law Z.

National approaches diverge markedly on reasoned awards. The American tradition discourages reasoned awards in commercial arbitration,[21] on the ground that a statement of reasons will 'identify targets for the losing party to attack'.[22] Arbitrators on the Continent, however, are accustomed to reasoned awards, either because they are required to give them in domestic arbitrations,[23] or because they fear that failure to state reasons will invite a claim of prejudice.

Optimum arbitration control mechanisms must moderate between the competing goals of finality and fairness by limiting non-recognition of awards to three grounds: (i) arbitrator bias or corruption; (ii) arbitrator excess of authority; and (iii) denial of one side's right to present its case. These suggested grounds for nullity leave many questions open. In particular, experience has shown how difficult it is to draw the thin line between an arbitrator's simple mistake (resulting in a 'bad award') and an award incompatible with the arbitrator's mission.[24] Notwithstanding these uncertainties, however, the principles proposed above provide a starting point from which to elaborate appropriate standards of review in tax arbitration.

B. Annulment Procedures

Once tax treaty partners have reached a consensus on grounds for non-recognition, they need to ask whether there should be a bi-national procedure for annulment of defective awards, or whether annulment should be left to national courts alone. The advantage of a bi-national annulment procedure is that it reduces the risk of inconsistent treatment of an award in different countries.

The World Bank's International Centre for the Settlement of Investment Disputes (ICSID) provides one model for a supra-national annulment proce-

21. For a case holding that under the US Arbitration Act arbitrators have no duty to explain the reasons for their award, see *Sobel* v. *Hertz Warner*, 469 F.2d 1211 (2d Cir. 1972).
22. Robert Coulson, *Business Arbitration* (4th ed. 1992) at page 30. Coulson adds that the 'AAA does not encourage such opinions [although if] both parties want an opinion . . . the AAA has no objection'.
23. *See* French *Nouveau Code de Procédure Civile*, Article 1471. The Swiss *Concordat sur l'Arbitrage*, Article 33(1)(e), also requires reasoned awards unless the parties have expressly waived this requirement.
24. *See* generally, William W. Park, 'The Lex Loci Arbitri and International Commercial Arbitration', 32 *Int'l & Comp. Law Quarterly* 21 (1983), pages 48 – 51.

dure.[25] In ICSID arbitration, the President of the World Bank can appoint a three member 'Ad Hoc Committee' to review a disputed award. Appointments are made from panels submitted by member states on a list kept with the ICSID Secretary General.

The North American Free Trade Agreement (NAFTA) also contain arbitration challenge procedures that are instructive for tax arbitration,[26] as did NAFTA's predecessor the Canada-U.S. Free Trade Agreement.[27] These Agreements provide that a bi-national panel from the exporting and importing states will review national antidumping and countervailing duty decisions. The decision of the bi-national panel in an anti-dumping or countervailing duty case can itself be reviewed by an 'Extraordinary Challenge Committee'. While the bi-national panel will apply the same standard of review as a court in the country whose decision is challenged,[28] the Extraordinary Challenge Committee will apply more limited 'supra-national' standards. Challenge will be permitted only for (i) gross misconduct, bias, or serious conflict of interest, (ii) a serious departure from a fundamental rule of procedure, or (iii) a manifest excess of the panel's jurisdiction.[29] In addition, it must be shown that the objectionable behavior 'has materially affected the panel's decision and threatens the integrity of the binational panel review'.

Not all international arbitral systems provide for uniform supra-national review of awards. Under the New York Arbitration Convention, for example, annulment of awards is left up to the national law of the arbitral situs. If an

25. For the text of the 'Washington Convention' establishing ICSID, *see* 575 UNTS 159. On ICSID generally, W. Michael Reisman, *Systems of Control in International Adjudication* (1992), Chapter 3, at 46 – 106; W. Michael Reisman, 'Repairing ICSID's Control System: Some Comments on Aaron Broches' 'Observations on the Finality of ICSID Awards',' 7 *ICSID Review* 196 (1992); W. Michael Reisman, 'The Breakdown of the Control Mechanism in ICSID Arbitration', 1989 *Duke Law Journal* 739; Moshe Hirsch, *The Arbitration Mechanisms of the International Centre for the Settlement of Investment Disputes* (1993); Georges Delaume, 'ICSID and the Courts', 77 *American J. of International Law* 784 (1983); Georges Delaume, 'ICSID Arbitration', in *Contemporary Problems in International Arbitration* 23 (J. Lew, ed. 1987).
26. NAFTA Chapter 19. *See* Homer Moyer, 'Chapter 19 of NAFTA: Binational Panels as Trade Courts of Last Resort', 27 *International Lawyer* 707 (1993); Gary Horlick and F. Amanda DeBusk, 'Dispute Resolution under NAFTA', 10 *Journal of International Arbitration* (No. 1) 51 (March 1993); Serge Gravel, 'Arbitration Within the NAFTA Area', 4 *ICC Court of Arbitration Bulletin* (No. 2) page 22 (October 1993). In addition, NAFTA contains a mechanism for dealing with disputes between the member states that are contracting parties to the treaty, as provision for investment disputes between a member state and an investor to be submitted for arbitration under the rules of ICSID or the United Nations Commission on International Trade Law (UNCITRAL). See NAFTA Chapter 11, Section B, Articles 1115 – 1139.
27. FTA Chapter 19, 27 ILM 281 (1988). *See* discussion of the 1991 'Fresh, Chilled and Frozen Pork Case' in Andreas Lowenfeld, 'The Free Trade Agreement Meets its First Challenge', 37 *McGill L.J.* 597 (1992).
28. For example, in the case of the United States this will be § 416A(b)(1)(B), Tariff Act of 1930 for the US. *See* 19 USC § 416A(b)(1)(B).
29. *See* Appendix I – 2.

award rendered in Paris is annulled by a French court, the Convention permits courts in New York to refuse recognition to the award. However, the grounds on which the award might be set aside would be determined by French arbitration law, not the New York Convention. In contrast, the 1961 European Convention on International Commercial Arbitration,[30] which complements the New York Convention in disputes among residents of European countries, permits refusal of recognition to an award annulled in another contracting state only if the annulment was for a Convention-enumerated reason.[31]

C. Multilateral Treaties and National Statutes

It remains an open question whether tax arbitration might already be covered by existing multilateral arbitration conventions and national arbitration statutes. Nothing would prevent a tax treaty from excluding tax awards from the coverage of such conventions and statutes. To date, however, treaties are silent on the matter.

1. Arbitration Treaties

The New York Convention covers foreign awards, which is to say, awards rendered outside the country where recognition is sought.[32] For example, an award rendered in the United States would be deemed foreign in Germany, and *vice-versa.*

The Convention explicitly gives contracting states the option to restrict its coverage to arbitrations 'arising out of legal relationships considered as commercial'. Many countries, including France, have decided *not* to limit the Convention's scope to commercial disputes.[33] Even in countries that have opted for the commercial limitation, transfer pricing disputes arguably 'arise out of' a commercial relationship when the origin of the dispute is a pricing arrangement contained in a commercial contract.

The Iranian Claims arbitrations in the Hague present an arbitral regime analogous to tax treaty arbitration, in the sense that they are established by inter-state treaty rather than the agreement of private individuals. United States courts have held that Iranian Claims awards fall within the scope of the

30. European Convention on International Commercial Arbitration, Geneva, 1961. 484 UNTS 349.
31. The grounds for annulment acceptable under the European Convention resemble the procedural defects set forth in first four defenses to enforcement of awards in Article V of the New York Convention, including an invalid arbitration agreement, lack of proper notice and arbitral excess of authority.
32. The Convention also covers awards that are 'non-domestic', although the precise meaning of the term is uncertain. *See* Bergesen v. Joseph Muller Corp., 710 F.2d 928 (2d Cir. 1983).
33. France has withdrawn its commercial exception reservation under the treaty. *See* 1990 *Revue de l'Arbitrage* at 210, noting Décret No. 90 – 170, 16 février 1990, publishing the French withdrawal letter to the United Nations dated 17 November 1989.

New York Convention.[34] The Second Circuit has expressly refused to enforce an Iranian Claims award where the arbitrator failed to give one party an adequate opportunity to present its case, and thus ran afoul of Article V of the New York Convention.[35]

One reason that it matters whether the New York Convention applies to tax arbitration is that the Convention enumerates grounds for non-recognition of awards. Most of these relate to procedural fairness, and are non-controversial. However, Article V(2)(b) of the Convention permits non-recognition of awards that violate the catch-all and malleable term 'public policy', which for reasons stated earlier could be dangerous to the health of tax arbitration.

2. National Arbitration Statutes

National arbitration laws in some cases may be drafted broadly enough to support an argument that tax arbitration is within their scope, at least as long as the relevant tax treaty is silent on the matter. Arbitration statutes do not necessarily restrict their coverage to agreements between private parties. For example, the French international arbitration decree covers arbitrations that 'implicate international commerce'.[36] Almost by definition, international transfer pricing disputes will 'implicate international commerce', since they arise from a sale, service or license between related entities in different countries.

In the Netherlands, commentators have suggested that Dutch arbitration law applies to awards rendered in the Netherlands purusant to an inter-state con-

34. *See Gould* v. *Iran*, 969 F.2d 764 (9th Cir. 1992), and Iran *Aircraft Industries v. Avco Corporation*, 980 F.2d 141 (2d Cir. 1992). Both cases arose out of cases in which Iran won arbitrations in the Hague and subsequently attempted to enforce the awards in the United States. On the Iranian Claims Tribunal, *see* generally David Caron, 'The Nature of the Iran-United States Claims Tribunal and the Evolving Structure of International Dispute Resolution', *American Journal of International Law* 104 (1990); Jamal Seifi, *Procedural Remedies Against Awards of the Iran-US. Claims Tribunal*, 8 *Arbitration International* (No. 1) 41.

35. In *Iran Aircraft* v. *Avco Corporation*, 980 F.2d 141 (2d Cir. 1992) the Court invoked a defense under Article V(1)(b) of the New York Convention, refusing to enforce the award precisely because the American defendant had been 'unable to present [its] case'. The arbitral tribunal had misled the defendant by stating that it would accept as evidence of claims an audited list of invoices rather than the actual invoices of amounts claimed, but in the end denied the claims because the originals were not presented. The Court expressly rejected the argument that the Iranian Claims award was 'directly' enforceable without passing through the strainer of New York Convention defenses. The Court rejected the argument that the award was to be given 'direct' enforceability, and stated 'The 'final and binding' language in the [Algiers] Accords does not bar consideration of the defenses to enforcement provided for in the New York Convention'. 980 F.2d 141, at 145.

36. NCPC Article 1492 states, 'Un arbitrage est international s'il implique le commerce international'.

vention.[37] One implication of such a conclusion is that Dutch courts could pronounce the nullity of tax treaty awards rendered within Dutch territory notwithstanding their 'public' character.

In the United States, tax awards might be implemented by a closing agreement, which under the Internal Revenue Code would not be final as to 'fraud or misfeasance'.[38] Moreover, the capacious scope of the Federal Arbitration Act covers any arbitration agreement contained in 'a contract evidencing a transaction involving [inter-state or international] commerce'.[39]

To meet a concern for undue national court interference in fiscal arbitration, tax treaties might explicitly exclude judicial review by national courts. Language to this effect could be modelled on Article 54(l) of the ICSID Convention, which provides that each contracting state shall recognize an ICSID award 'as if it were a final judgment of a court in that state'.[40]

II. A Case Study of Transfer Pricing Arbitration

A. Tax Court Rule 124

The American experience with tax arbitration, limited as it may be, points to areas of potential concern in connection with control mechanisms. Tax Court Rule 124 permits a factual controversy to be resolved by arbitration if the IRS

37. *See* e.g., Albert Jan van den Berg, 'Proposed Dutch Law on the Iran-US Claims Settlement Declaration', *International Business Lawyer* (September 1984) 341 at 342: 'It is a generally accepted rule in international arbitration that the law applicable to the arbitration in principle means the law of arbitration of the country where the arbitration takes place. . . In this case, the UNCITRAL Rules (Article 1, paragraph 2) imply that Dutch arbitration law is applicable'. Professor van den Berg commented in the context of 1983 draft legislation introduced in the lower house of the Dutch Parliament which would have limited Dutch court actions to nullify Iranian Claims awards to cases where the proceedings showed a manifest breach of the principles of proper administration of justice (which is another way of saying procedural due process) or where the award is manifestly contrary to public order. *See* Dutch Lower House of Parliament, 1982 – 83, Bill No. 18.000. The law was withdrawn due to political maneuvering. Mr. van den Berg was favorable to the proposed law as a way to reduce uncertainties regarding the law applicable to the proceedings. Compare L. Hardenberg, 'The Awards of the Iran-US Claims Tribunal', *International Business Lawyer* (September 1984), at 337, opposing the proposed Dutch Iranian Claims law as incompatible with the Algiers Claims Settlement Declaration. *See* generally, William T. Lake and Jane Tucker Dana, 'Judicial Review of Awards of the Iran-United States Claims Tribunal: Are the Tribunal's Awards Dutch?' 16 *Law and Policy in International Business* 755 (1984).
38. IRC Section 7121(b).
39. 9 USC § 2. Commercial arbitration in the United States relies on different statutory underpinnings than labor arbitration. The former rests on Title 9 of the US Code; the predicate for the latter is a case known as *Textile Workers* v. *Lincoln Mills*, 353 US 448 (1957), based on Section 301 of the Taft-Hartley Act.
40. Convention on the Settlement of Investment Disputes Between States and Nationals of Other States, Article 54(l).

and the taxpayer agree to enter into a stipulation containing at least five components: (i) the issues to be resolved, (ii) the identity of the arbitrators or the procedure to be used in selecting the arbitrator, (iii) the manner of payment of the arbitrator, (iv) a prohibition against *ex parte* communication with the arbitrator and (v) an agreement to be bound by the arbitrator's findings.[41] The stipulation may also delineate other matters the parties 'deem to be appropriate', which might include, for example, a more detailed specification of the type of arbitral procedure to be followed.

In some ways domestic tax arbitration may have a closer family resemblance to court litigation than to commercial arbitration. The latter usually unfolds without any judicial intervention. However, arbitration under Tax Court Rule 124 originates in an action in the Tax Court, which is involved in the arbitral procedure from its initiation until confirmation of the award in the form of a judgment.

B. The Apple Case

One stipulation under Tax Court Rule 124 was reached in a well-publicized inter-company transfer pricing dispute involving Apple Computer[42]. The basic controversy related to income of the Singapore branch of Apple International, which manufactured printed circuit boards.[43] The Internal Revenue Service sought to reallocate income from Apple Singapore to Apple US, based on its view of arm's length prices on transactions that included sales, services and the use of intangibles.[44] The parties' stipulation provided that each side would be 'limited to presenting to the [arbitral] panel only *one* amount [that Singapore would have earned at arm's length prices] for each taxable year in dispute' and that the Panel would have to select 'one of the [two] amounts

41. The text of Rule 124 can be found in 2 Bender's Federal Tax Service TR-124 or [1993] 12 CCH Standard Federal Tax Reporter, Paragraph 42,983.50 at page 71,200. On American tax arbitration, *see* generally Kirsten McDonough, *Resolving federal Tax Disputes Through ADR*, 48 ARBITRATION JOURNAL (June 1993) at page 38.
42. The dispute covered the tax years 1984, 1985 and 1986. The case had been brought before Judge Julian Jacobs in the US Tax Court. *See* generally IRS News Release IR 92 – 20, 6 March 1992, printed in [1992] 13 CCH Standard Federal Tax Reporter, ¶ 46,217 at page 76,949. The parties stipulated that the three-member arbitral tribunal would consist of a retired judge, an economist and an industry expert. The arbitrators were Paul Adler, a professor of business at the University of Southern California, retired judge Nicholas Bua and John Shoven, Director of the Center for Economic Policy Research at Stanford.
43. In its deficiency notice the IRS originally sought an allocation of $114 million. The stipulation stated that the range of possible income for Apple Singapore was between $16.3 million and $130.9 million.
44. *Apple Computer Inc. and Consolidated Subsidiaries v. Commissioner of Internal Revenue,* Docket No. 21781 – 90, Stipulation for Resolution of Issue Through Voluntary Binding Arbitration Under Tax Rule 124.

presented by the parties . . .'.[45] The arbitrators unanimously decided that the income of Apple Computer Inc. (US) should be increased by $76 million, pursuant to the allocations submitted by the Internal Revenue Service.[46]

In the Apple arbitration a dispute arose almost immediately about the scope of the arbitrators' authority concerning transactions involving an Apple company in Ireland. Apple argued that the Irish transactions were outside the scope of the submission to arbitration. The Tax Court was asked to hear a motion for clarification on the arbitrators' authority on this point.[47]

The arbitral procedure chosen in the Apple case is sometimes called 'baseball arbitration', because of its use to set the compensation of major league baseball players in the United States.[48] The arbitrators must pick from either of two figures that represent each party's 'last best offer'. Baseball arbitration is said to result in a high number of pre-arbitration settlements by encouraging each side to move toward a middle ground. A party that submits an unreasonably high or low figure risks having its position rejected, leaving the other side's submission as the only alternative.[49]

The parties in American tax arbitration are not required to use baseball procedures. They can also opt for the same process used in normal commercial arbitration, where the arbitrators generally are free to make an award in whatever amount they deem correct, as long as they stay within the scope of their jurisdiction.

45. Stipulation Article III(A).
46. *See* Stipulation of Adjustments Arising from Arbitration Panel Findings, signed 20 September and 22 September, and filed with Tax Court on 22 September 1993. *See also* BNA Daily Report for Executives, 27 September 1993, 1993 DER 185 d 59, Section on Taxation, Section G, 185. The amounts were $ 19,987,000 for 1984, $ 21,620,000 for 1985 and $ 34,936,000 for 1986. Apple subsequently filed a petition for reduction of its income. *See* petitions in Docket No. 21781 – 90 filed on 27 September and 29 November 1993.
47. *See Apple Computer v. Commissioner,* Tax Court, motion in Action No. 21781 – 90 filed on 4 May 1993.
48. Since 1974, the Basic Agreement between the major league Baseball Players Association and the club owners provides for resolution of salary disputes under 'last best offer' arbitration. *See* American Arbitration Association, 'Using Alternative Dispute Resolution to Settle Sports Disputes', at pages 8 – 11. *See* generally, John S. Murray, Alan Scott Rau and Edward F. Sherman, *Processes of Dispute Resolution: The Role of Lawyers* (1989), at 591 – 601.
49. In 1993 there was an 85% settlement rate in major league American baseball cases. Of the hundred and eighteen (118) players who went to arbitration, six (6) won, twelve (12) lost and one hundred (100) settled by negotiations before the award. *See* 'Wrapping up Arbitration', *New York Times,* 22 February 1993, page 2; 'No Sacrifice for Players in Arbitration Hearings', *Chicago Tribune,* 22 February 1993, page 9; M. Noble, 'Players Cash In Big-Time', *Newsday,* 21 February 1993, page 8.

III. Drafting a Tax Arbitration Agreement

Courts and bi-national panels that implement control mechanisms inevitably will look to the parties' arbitration agreement in determining questions related to claims of arbitrator excess of authority, one of the principal grounds for non-recognition of awards. It is therefore vital that tax lawyers devote careful attention to drafting detailed terms of reference to cover arbitration of transfer pricing disputes.[50]

Five elements are essential to an international arbitration clause: (i) applicable procedural rules, either *ad hoc* or institutional; (ii) the mechanism for fixing the arbitrators' fees; (iii) the place of arbitration; (iv) the language of the arbitration; and (v) the number of arbitrators. In the context of tax arbitration, three elements likely to require special attention are fees, the number of arbitrators and procedural rules, all of which are discussed below.

A. Arbitrators' Fees

Calculation of the arbitrators' fees has been approached in two different ways: (i) an hourly or daily rate, or (ii) a percentage of the amount in dispute. The London Court of International Arbitration, for example, generally gives arbitrators between £ 600 and £ 2000 for each day of meetings, and between £ 150 and £ 375 per hour for other time spent.[51] In contrast, the International Chamber of Commerce sets maximum and minimum fee limits based on the amount in dispute, calculated at a different rate applicable to each successive slice of the amount in dispute.[52]

In tax arbitration, there is no consensus on whether the costs of arbitration should be paid by the taxpayer, the governments, or both the governments and

50. On drafting arbitration clauses, *see* generally W. Laurence Craig, William W. Park, Jan A.S. Paulsson, *International Chamber of Commerce Arbitration* (2d ed. 1990) chapters 5 – 9; J. Stewart McClendon, 'Arbitration Clauses in International Contracts', in *Survey of International Arbitration Sites* (J.S. McClendon, ed., 3rd ed., 1993), p. 127; Robert Coulson, 'The Practical Advantages of Administered Arbitration', *NIDR Forum* (Winter 1993), p. 41; Piero Bernardini, 'The Arbitration Clause of an International Contract', 9 *Journal of International Arbitration* (No, 2) 45 (1992); Michael F. Hoellering, 'How to Draft an AAA Arbitration Clause', 1991 – 92 *Arbitration and the Law* 166 (1992); Stephen R. Bond, 'How to Draft an ICC Arbitration Clause', 7 *ICSID Review – Foreign Investment Law Journal* 153 (1992); International Chamber of Commerce, *Working Group on the ICC Standard Arbitration Clause, Final Report*, Commission on International Arbitration, 1991 (Document No. 420/318 Rev.).

51. In the *Apple* case arbitrators fees were based on a 'reasonable' hourly rate. *See* discussion *supra* in Part II.

52. The percentages run from the 1.5% to 10% range at the bottom, to a range of .01% to .05% on amounts in excess of $100 million. For example, when the amount in controversy is $1 million, the fees of each arbitrator vary between $8,450 and $47,500; in a $5 million arbitration, the spread is from $17,450 to $96,500; for a $100 million dispute the minimum fee is $52,450 and the maximum $231,500.

the taxpayers. The 1984 Resolution of the International Chamber of Commerce on tax arbitration suggested that the governments should pay, because (in the words of the International Chamber of Commerce) the governments 'have not found a solution to the problem by ordinary means'.[53]

In the *Apple* case, the IRS and Apple agreed that each would bear half the costs, although neither party was responsible for the defaulting party's share. By contrast, in ICC arbitration when one side refuses to pay its advance on costs, the other side must pick up the difference in order to unblock the proceedings.

B. Number of Arbitrators

Whether disputes should be decided by a sole arbitrator or by a three member tribunal will depend on the factual configuaration of each case. A single arbitrator would normally be cheaper. However, there is a good argument that a three-member tribunal makes for a more rigorous decision-making process. Most people behave differently in groups than they do alone. Arbitrators, so the argument runs, will be less prone to sloppy decision-making if they must justify their reasoning in deliberations with two other professionals.

C. Procedural Rules

Tax arbitration may be conducted on either an *ad hoc* or a supervised basis.[54] The latter presents the advantage of supplying an institution to move along a recalcitrant party inclined to drag its feet. *Ad hoc* arbirtration can be tailor-made by the parties, or can follow the rules drafted by the United Nations Commission on International Trade Law (UNCITRAL). In the *Apple* arbitration the parties stipulated that American Arbitration Association rules would apply only in the event that there was a gap in the stipulation.[55]

In addition to a basic procedural framework, parties to tax arbitration should give thought to the methods for proving their case that they consider appropriate. In the *Apple* Stipulation, for example, the parties stated that each side would have the right to direct examination and cross-examination of witnesses.[56] Civil and commercial judicial proceedings in Europe tend to rely more heavily on documents than Anglo-American legal actions. Many observers of arbitration are betting that the Continental model will ultimately become the rule in international proceedings.

53. International Chamber of Commerce, 'Resolution of International Tax Conflicts', ICC Doc. 180/240, reprinted in 1984 IBFD European Taxation 337, at 339.
54. For example, the supervisory institution might be the American Arbitration Association, the International Chamber of Commerce or the London Court of International Arbitration.
55. *See* Apple Stipulation, *supra*, at Clause II-C.
56. *See* Apple Stipulation, *supra*, at Clause VIII-D-3.

Conclusion

The success of tax treaty arbitration will depend in large measure on the type of control mechanisms adopted to guide arbitrators and to enhance uniformity in treaty interpretation. In contrast to settlement of commercial disputes, where arbitration or settlement usually takes place in the shadow of potential court actions, adjudication of differences arising under tax treaties will be subject to no neutral courts with compulsory jurisdiction over the two states.

While the arbitrators' decision on the merits of a transfer pricing dispute should be final, this does not mean that international tax awards should be completely free from review. Respect for procedural integrity requires that tax awards subject to challenge on at least three grounds: (1) arbitrator bias or corruption; (2) arbitrator excess of authority; and (3) denial of one side's right to present its case.

To further consistency in application of these criteria, the nullity of an award should be determined under bi-national challenge procedures rather than on an *ad hoc* basis by national courts. In this manner, an arbitral process that balances fairness and finality will be able to play an increasingly important role in resolving fiscal disputes that might otherwise lead to a destructive level of economic double taxation.

Appendix

Illustrative Treaty and Statutory Provisions:
Non-recognition and Annulment of Awards

A. Treaties
1. New York Convention of 1958
2. Canada-US Free Trade Agreement
3. International Centre for the Settlement of Investment Disputes (ICSID)
4. International Law Commission Draft on Arbitral Procedure
5. Geneva Convention of 1961 (European Convention)

B. National Statutes
1. England
2. France
3. Switzerland
4. United States
5. UN Commission on International Trade Law

A. Treaties

1. Convention on the Recognition and Enforcement of Foreign Arbitral Awards[57]

Article V

1. Recognition and enforcement of the award may be refused, at the request of the party against whom it is invoked, only if that party furnishes to the competent authority where the recognition and enforcement is sought, proof that:

(a) The parties to the agreement were, under the law applicable to them, un-

57. 10 June 1958, 21 UST 2517, 2520, 330 UNTS 38, 40–42.

der some incapacity, or the said agreement is not valid under the law to which the parties have subjected it or, failing any indication thereon, under the law of the country where the award was made; or

(b) The party against whom the award is invoked was not given proper notice of the appointment of the arbitrator or of the arbitration proceedings or was otherwise unable to present his case; or

(c) The award deals with a difference not contemplated by or not falling within the terms of the submission to arbitration, or it contains decisions on matters beyond the scope of the submission to arbitration, provided that, if the decisions on matters submitted to arbitration can be separated from those not so submitted, that part of the award which contains decisions on matters submitted to arbitration may be recognized and enforced; or

(d) The composition of the arbitral authority or the arbitral procedure was not in accordance with the agreement of the parties, or, failing such agreement, was not in accordance with the law of the country where the arbitration took place; or

(e) The award has not yet become binding on the parties, or has been set aside or suspended by a competent authority of the country in which, or under the law of which, that award was made.

2. Recognition and enforcement of an arbitral award may also be refused if the competent authority in the country where recognition and enforcement is sought finds that:

(a) The subject matter of the difference is not capable of settlement by arbitration under the law of that country; or

(b) The recognition or enforcement of the award would be contrary to the public policy of that country.

2. North American Free Trade Agreement (NAFTA)[58]

Article 1904, paragraph 13, sets forth as follows the grounds for review of a decision by a bi-national panel on countervailing duties and anti-dumping. Other NAFTA dispute resolution mechanisms are discussed in the text of this article, *supra* at Section I-B.

> Where, within a reasonable time after the panel decision is issued, a party alleges that:
>
> (a)(i) a member of the panel was guilty of gross misconduct, bias, or a serious conflict of interest, or otherwise materially violated the rules of conduct,
>
> (ii) the panel seriously departed from a fundamental rule of procedure, or

58. 32 ILM. 605 (1993).

(iii) the panel manifestly exceeded its powers, authority or jurisdiction, for example by failing to apply the appropriate standard of review, and

(b) any of the actions set out in subparagraph (a) has materially affected the panel's decision and threatens the integrity of the binational panel review process,

that party may avail itself of the extraordinary challenge procedure.

3. Convention on the Settlement of Investment Disputes Between States and Nationals of Other States[59]

Article 52

Either party may request annulment of the award by an application in writing addressed to the Secretary-General on one or more of the following grounds:

(a) that the Tribunal was not properly constituted;
(b) that the Tribunal has manifestly exceeded its powers;
(c) that there was corruption on the part of a member of the Tribunal;
(d) that there has been a serious departure from a fundamental rule of procedure; or
(e) that the award has failed to state the reasons on which it is based.

4. International Law Commission Model Draft Treaty on Arbitral Procedure[60]

Article 36

The validity of an award may be challenged by either party on one or more of the following grounds:

(a) That the tribunal has exceeded its powers;
(b) That there was corruption on the part of a member of the tribunal;
(c) That there has been a serious departure from a fundamental rule of procedure, including total or partial failure to state the reasons for the award.

59. 18 March 1965, 17 UST 1270, 1290–91, 575 UNTS 159, 192.

60. These draft principles apply to 'any undertaking to have recourse to arbitration in order to settle a dispute between States'. International Law Commission, Documents of the Tenth Session, [1958] 2 YB Int'l L. Comm'n 15, UN Doc. A/CN.4/113, Article 36 (1958 version of the 1953 Draft).

5. European Convention on International Arbitration[61]

Article IX

1. The setting aside in a Contracting State of an arbitral award covered by this Convention shall only constitute a ground for the refusal of recognition or enforcement in another Contracting State where such setting aside took place in a State in which, or under the law of which, the award has been made and for one of the following reasons:

(a) the parties to the arbitration agreement were under the law applicable to them, under some incapacity or the said agreement is not valid under the law to which the parties have subjected it or, failing any indication thereon, under the law of the country where the award was made, or
(b) the party requesting the setting aside of the award was not given proper notice of the appointment of the arbitrator or of the arbitration proceedings or was otherwise unable to present his case; or
(c) the award deals with a difference not contemplated by or not falling within the terms of the submission to arbitration, or it contains decisions on matters beyond the scope of the submission to arbitration, provided that, if the decisions on matters submitted to arbitration can be separated from those not so submitted, that part of the award which contains decisions on matters submitted to arbitration need not be set aside;
(d) the composition of the arbitral authority or the arbitral procedure was not in accordance with the agreement of the parties, or failing such agreement, with the provisions of Article IV of this Convention.

B. Illustrative National Statutes

1. England

Section 23(2) of the 1950 Arbitration Act[62]

Where an arbitrator or umpire has misconducted himself or the proceed-

61. Geneva, 21 April 1961. 484 UNTS 349, 374–76. Article IX goes on to provide that in relations between Contracting States that are also parties to the New York Convention this Article limits the application of Article V(1)(e) of the New York Convention (refusal of recognition to awards set aside where rendered) solely to the cases of setting aside set out under European Convention Article IX.
62. 14 Geo. 6. c. 27.

ings, or an arbitration or award has been improperly procured, the High Court may set the award aside.

2. France

Article 1502, Nouveau code de procédure civile[63]

An appeal against a decision granting recognition or enforcement may be brought only in the following cases:

1. If the arbitrator decided in the absence of an arbitration agreement or on the basis of a void or expired agreement;
2. If the arbitral tribunal was irregularly composed or the sole arbitrator irregularly appointed;
3. If the arbitrator decided in a manner incompatible with the mission conferred upon him;
4. If due process [literally, '*le principe de la contraction*', or the principle of an adversarial process'] was not respected;
5. If recognition or enforcement would be contrary to international public policy ['*ordre public international*'].

3. Switzerland

Article 190(2), Loi sur le droit international privé[64]

[The award] can only be set aside where:

a. a sole arbitrator has been incorrectly appointed or the arbitral tribunal has been incorrectly constituted;
b. the arbitral tribunal has wrongly declared itself to have or not to have jurisdiction;
c. the arbitral tribunal has decided on claims which were not submitted to it or has omitted to decide on any claim submitted to it;
d. the principles of the equality of treatment of the parties and their right to be heard in a contested proceeding have not been observed;
e. the award is incompatible with public policy.

63. Translation by W. Laurence Craig, William W. Park and Jan A.S. Paulsson; *see* Craig, Park and Paulsson, *International Chamber of Commerce Arbitration* (2d ed. 1990), Chapter 30.
64. 18 December 1987, entered into force 1 January 1989. Translation by Adam Samuel. Article 192 of the Swiss statute goes on to provide that when neither party to the arbitration is a Swiss resident, challenge to awards can be excluded by an express statement ('*déclaration expresse*'). In disputes exclusively between Swiss parties, judicial review of arbitral awards in Switzerland will be governed by the Inter-cantonal Arbitration Concordat, which permits challenge *inter alia* for 'arbitrariness', defined to include 'clear violations of law or equity'.

4. United States

Section 10, Federal Arbitration Act[65]

In either of the following cases the United States court in and for the district wherein the award was made may make an order vacating the award upon the application of any party to the arbitration –

(a) Where the award was procured by corruption, fraud, or undue means.
(b) Where there was evident partiality or corruption in the arbitrators, or either of them.
(c) Where the arbitrators were guilty of misconduct in refusing to postpone the hearing, upon sufficient cause shown, or in refusing to hear evidence pertinent and material to the controversy; or of any other misbehavior by which the rights of any party have been prejudiced.
(d) Where the arbitrators exceeded their powers, or so imperfectly executed them that a mutual, final, and definite award upon the subject matter submitted was not made.

5. Uncitral Model Law on International Commercial Arbitration[66]

Article 34(2)

An arbitral award may be set aside by the appropriate court specified in Article 6 only if:

(a) the party making the application furnishes proof that:
    i. a party to the arbitration agreement referred to in article 7 was under some incapacity; or the said agreement is not valid under the law to which the parties have subjected it or, failing any indication thereon, under the law of this State; or
    ii. the party making the application was not given proper notice of the appointment of an arbitrator or of the arbitral proceedings or was otherwise unable to present his case; or
    iii. the award deals with a dispute not contemplated by or not falling within the terms of the submission to arbitration, or contains decisions on matters beyond the scope of the submission to arbitration, provided that, if the decisions on matters submitted to arbitration can be separated from those not so submitted, only that part of the award which contains decisions on matters not submitted to arbitration may be set aside; or

65. 9 USC § 10.
66. UN Commission on International Trade Law, 21 June 1985, UN Doc. No. A/40/17 (Annex I).

iv. the composition of the arbitral tribunal or the arbitral procedure was not in accordance with the agreement of the parties, unless such agreement was in conflict with a provision of this Law from which the parties cannot derogate, or, failing such agreement, was not in accordance with this Law; or

(b) the court finds that:

i. the subject-matter of the dispute is not capable of settlement by arbitration under the law of this State; or

ii. the award is in conflict with the public policy of this State.

SEVEN POINTS FOR AN INDEPENDENT ARBITRATION PROCEDURE IN INTERNATIONAL TAX CONFLICTS

Professor Wolfgang Ritter

1. The struggle for revenue between states is increasing instead of decreasing. The troublesome tendencies of the new US-American regulations for international transfer pricing as well as the adamant insistence on behalf of US States on an internationally unsuitable unitary taxation or recent development in Korean taxation of sales activities make this preoccupyingly clear.

2. Within this scenery the danger for the tax payer increases, so that he becomes object of tax conflicts between states, a situation which he cannot avoid even by the most scrupulous setting of this business situation for tax purposes.

3. This development clearly contradicts the fact that the internationalization of economic relations is getting more and more necessary for the national economies concerned and that the international cooperation between the tax administrations becomes closer and closer.

4. With the mutual agreement procedure, the international tax treaties offer a way to protect the tax payer from double or even multiple taxation. However, the success of this procedure is bound to the willingness of the states concerned to keep to the law and to reach appropriate solutions. The more the financial needs of the states dominate their opinions on what is seen as legally binding and appropriate, the greater becomes the danger that the tax payer's protection disappears.

5. Such misdevelopment can only be avoided by giving the tax payer the right, in case of failure of a mutual agreement procedure, to provoke a decision by independent judgement, which is also binding upon the states concerned. States which already contemplate the possibility of such independent arbitration in their treaties should consider it a nobile officium, to make the widest possible use of this possibility.

6. The continuing resistance of many states against such independent arbitration can by no means be defended. Moreover the sovereignty of states cannot be a reason for refusing the tax payer legal protection, which is a fundamental right in any modern state.

7. A mandatory arbitration procedure depending on the demand of the tax payer, will compel the states to draw their legal positions together rather than letting them drift apart, and in case of conflict, to find solutions which make additional arbitration procedures avoidable.

In conclusion, an independent arbitration procedure on demand of the tax payer is to become an inevitable foundation stone for an international peace order for taxation.

SUMMARY OF PROCEEDINGS OF THE SEMINAR 'RESOLUTION OF TAX TREATY CONFLICTS BY ARBITRATION'

written by Dr. Barry Bracewell-Milnes (UK) on the occasion of the 47th Congress, Florence 1993 (7 October); available only in English

Professor Gustav Lindencrona, Sweden, Chairman of the Seminar, welcomed the participants. He said that there had been a breakthrough in the recognition of arbitration during the last few years: five treaties had been signed, in addition to the European Community Convention. There had been no cases so far; but the texts of these documents were important in their own right. Among the papers made available to participants in the Seminar were his own background note and outline of the Seminar; the European Community Arbitration Convention; extracts from the German/Swedish double tax treaty, the German/United States double tax treaty, the French/German double tax treaty, the Dutch/United States double tax treaty and the Mexican/United States double tax treaty; an International Chamber of Commerce paper on the resolution of international tax conflicts; and Article 25 (Mutual Agreement Procedure) of the OECD Double Tax Convention. In the outline of the Seminar discussion, the topic was divided into three parts: a description of recent experience; principal and practical problems in the creation of an arbitration procedure; and future developments. The first of these three topics (a description of recent experience) would not be taken at this morning's Seminar but would be left for any published version of its Proceedings. The second topic (problems in the creation of an arbitration procedure) had been divided into sub-sections and would be discussed in detail by the Panel. The third topic (future developments) would provide an opportunity to deploy arguments for and against various possible outcomes. He introduced the Members of his Panel, who were: Dr. Alfred Burckhardt, Switzerland; Professor Mario Burgio, Italy; Professor Luc Hinnekens, Belgium; Professor William Park, United States; Professor Wolfgang Ritter, Germany; Dr. Giuseppe Marino, Italy, who was Secretary of the Panel. Professor Lindencrona offered a definition of arbitration: a procedure where competent authorities were not the only participants and where decisions were taken by an independent party rather than by a court.

Professor Lindencrona opened the discussion of section II (principal and practical problems in the creation of an arbitration procedure) with his own consideration of the question whether arbitration should be mandatory or not. The discussion of arbitration as a method of solving tax treaty conflicts was based on the assumption that a preceding mutual agreement procedure had not been successful. The taxpayer had thus applied to the competent authority in the country of which he was a resident. The competent authority had found his application justified and started negotiations with the competent authority in the other contracting state in order to find a solution; but no solution had been found, because the competent authorities held different views of the matter. Moreover, even if there was a prospect of the competent authorities' reaching an agreement, the procedure was extremely time-consuming. The main differences between an arbitration procedure and a mutual agreement procedure were that an arbitration award was made by an independent group of arbitrators and that a decision should always be reached. If the arbitrators could not agree, the decision was taken by a majority vote. Furthermore, an arbitration award was always based on law, be it treaty provisions or general principles of international tax law; if the arbitrators tried to find a solution *ex aequo et bono*, it was not an arbitration procedure. The first problem in the creation of an arbitration procedure was whether it should be mandatory or not. By a mandatory procedure was meant a procedure that should take place if the competent authorities were not able to reach a mutual agreement as a result of a difference of opinion or if the competent authorities had not been able to find a solution within a certain prescribed time limit. A non-mandatory procedure meant merely that both the contracting parties must agree that an arbitration procedure should take place. The double tax treaties which had so far introduced arbitration clauses had not made the arbitration procedure mandatory. Both the German/Swedish and the German/United States treaties 'made agreement between the parties a prerequisite for the conflict's being submitted to arbitration'. The only difference was that the German/Swedish treaty spoke about the contracting states and the German/United States treaty about the competent authorities. The additional protocol to the French/German treaty had a time limit of twenty-four months but still did not make arbitration mandatory. The Netherlands/United States treaty required that both competent authorities and the taxpayer or even that taxpayers should agree to submit the conflict to arbitration. It was only the European Community Arbitration Convention which had a procedure which might be called mandatory. It was thus clear that even states which had opened the way to an arbitration procedure had been very cautious and had hesitated to make this procedure mandatory. However, Professor Lindencrona considered that there were strong arguments for a mandatory procedure containing a provision that if the parties had not been able to reach mutual agreement within a prescribed and not excessive period of time the conflict should be submitted to arbitration. The main arguments were: (1) if the arbitration procedure was not mandatory, the problem was essentially the same as under the mutual agreement procedure, namely that there was no guarantee that a solution would be found in every conflict; (2) a mandatory procedure, especially if combined with a time limit, would take less time than mutual agreement procedures, which often took far too long. In any case, an arbitration procedure, even if not mandatory, was better than no arbitration procedure at all: arbitration meant that the conflict would be solved by an award and that the solution would be based on law, namely the law of the tax treaty.

Professor Ritter said that there was a natural progression from the mutual agreement procedure through a claim by a taxpayer to the resolution of conflicts by arbitration. There was a certain irony in states' being reluctant to accept arbitration, given that at the domestic level it was normal for disputed cases to go from court to court on appeal. Within the European Community, the taxpayer's agreement was required to make the arbitration decision mandatory; in this contex the taxpayer was sovereign.

This led to the discussion of the second topic under section (II) - the position of the taxpayer. Professor Hinnekens said that a mutual agreement procedure was between two contracting states; but in international tax arbitration the position of the taxpayer had to be recognised. The arbitral award bound not only the competent authorities of the two states but also the taxpayer, who might not even have the right to appeal from it. The taxpayer thus had an unavoidable and legitimate interest in the procedure, which must be recognised by making him practically a party thereto almost in the same manner as in a court procedure. Thus international tax arbitration should be characterised by the following.

- The taxpayer's right of initiative. The taxpayer had the right to present his case and the competent authority responsible for initiating the procedure might not refuse to do so. It must set the procedure in motion unless the complaint was clearly abusive.
- No abuse of escape clauses by the competent authority. For instance, the competent authority might not refuse to take the case because it would fall outside the scope of the convention pursuant to a clearly unreasonable interpretation of its terms. It might also not refuse to take the case by filing criminal or administrative complaints against the taxpayer.
- The taxpayer's right to a reasonable time framework. This might be something between three months and three years.
- The taxpayer's right to provide any information and documentation which he deemed to be of use to his case.
- The taxpayer's right to refute the arguments of the revenue authorities.
- The taxpayer's right to appear or be represented before the arbitrators.
- The taxpayer's right to refuse to supply information and documentation requested by the arbitral commission if it was not obtainable under domestic law or administrative practice or if would disclose any trade or business secret.
- The taxpayer's right to information and access to reports of earlier arbitral awards.
- An obligation to secrecy on the part of the members of the arbitral commission. This raised the problem whether the same representatives of the authorities sitting on the arbitral commission and involved in parallel or subsequent administrative or criminal proceedings in the same case would or could forget

matters which they learned in the course of the arbitral proceedings and thus whether the same revenue representatives might be involved in both procedures.

- The taxpayer's right to a fair allocation of the costs of the procedure.
- The requirement that the arbitrators should be independent.
- The payment of interest on late tax payments or late tax refunds.
- The right of recourse to the remedies and procedures available under domestic law.
- The right to appeal from the arbitral decision. Such appeals were important where the taxpayer's legal position was not adequately recognised. In the European Community Convention the arbitral decision was not reviewable by any domestic court, in accordance with its level of international jurisdiction and by contrast with the mutual agreement procedure, which had no jurisdiction but only diplomatic force and effect.

Dr. Burckhardt said that the taxpayer must have the right to refute arguments advanced by the tax administrations. Professor Ritter said that the taxpayer should be able to challenge bias on the part of the tax authorities.

Professor Lindencrona opened the discussion of the third topic in section (II): how should the arbitrators be chosen? The arbitration commission could be appointed on an *ad hoc* basis when a conflict had arisen; but it could be argued that the establishment of an arbitration institute with experienced arbitrators and technical services would facilitate the arbitration procedure. There were also other possible solutions; for example, the arbitrators should be drawn from a group of experienced persons chosen beforehand. What were the advantages and disadvantages of these various methods? He invited Dr. Burckhardt to speak.

Dr. Burckhardt said that there were three questions at issue: How should the arbitral tribunal be constituted? What qualifications should its members possess? How and by whom should its members be chosen? The arbitral tribunal should consist of an odd number of members expert in the law of treaties and also conversant with the economics of the line of business concerned. It was important to avoid the unfortunate precedent of commercial arbitration, where arbitrators were chosen from a small pool of specialists in arbitration. Real fairness could not be achieved unless the arbitrators were, and were seen to be, independent and not susceptible to outside pressure. Thus, if people from the tax administration were to be appointed as arbitrators, they should at least be relieved of any obligation to report to or accept instructions from the revenue departments. Turning to the question of the appointment of arbitrators, he said that it was important that the bodies choosing the arbitrators should be really independent. Where there were three arbitrators, the appointment of the third was particularly difficult. The international Chamber of Commerce had a record of success in appointing experts in accountancy, economics and related disciplines to commercial arbitration tribunals; but the revenue departments would wish to retain control. Professor Burgio said that the appointment of the

Chairman of the arbitration tribunal was of critical importance. A system of indirect appointment such as had just been described was no certain guarantee of success.

Professor Lindencrona opened the discussion of the first three topics to the floor, and the following were the principal points made:

1. The mutual agreement procedure had proved a good means of reaching agreement. No cases were outstanding in Norway.
2. It had to be asked just why it was that governments were sometimes unable to find solutions to the matters of dispute between them. The answer was that they were sovereign states disagreeing over questions in which each thought that it had vital interests at stake.
3. It was the citizen or taxpayer who was the prime mover in attempting to resolve disputes between governments. He had the right to object to taxes being levied on him; but had he the right to an answer if there was no mutual agreement procedure?
4. The Panel could have looked more closely at the European Community Convention. This Convention was restricted to, questions of fact, whereas the emphasis in the Panel had been on questions of law. Under the European Community Convention it was mandatory to relieve double taxation arising from transfer pricing.

Professor Lindencrona introduced topic four of section(II): the relation between the arbitration award and national tax law. This relationship was complicated in some countries where even a mutual agreement sometimes could not be implemented for constitutional and other reasons. It was important to find solutions to such problems, since there would otherwise be an imbalance in the obligations of the two contracting states. Was the arbitration procedure a procedure between states or between tax administrations? The arbitration procedure (like the mutual agreement procedure) was in some respects an alternative to a national tax court procedure. Should the taxpayer be able to choose between the two procedures? It was intolerable that a national court procedure should preclude mutual agreement or arbitration. There must be a change of outlook: competent authorities had the authority of their states, and they must not have a status below that of national courts. There were also practical considerations: diplomats were not tax experts.

Professor Hinnekens said that there were two different remedies or procedures for resolving the same tax dispute (adjustment of profit in cases of transfer pricing). There was the national procedure between the enterprise and its own tax authority and there was the international procedure involving both tax authorities. The two procedures were in competition with one another in so far as the latter gave the taxpayer a second opportunity. He proposed four rules or principles for the orderly co-existence of these two procedures. First, convention arbitration rules prevailed over the less far-reaching obligations of the revenue authorities under domestic laws. Second, where the international procedure suffered from insufficient regulation, it was completed and amplified by reference to the rules of the national procedure. Third, convention rules might be permissive and allow the competent authorities to depart from them or defer their application. Fourth, the convention did not preclude the fulfilment by the competent authorities of their wider obligations under domestic law or treaty law. In other words, the convention set only minimum standards. For example, a case for the elimination of double taxation was still open if the convention time limit for presenting it had expired, but not the time limit in the bilateral treaty or national law.

Professor Lindencrona opened the discussion of the fifth topic under section (II), control mechanisms and award finality. Even if arbitral awards were final and binding on the substantive merits of the dispute, most arbitral régimes provided that courts might refuse to implement awards based on certain procedural defects which had traditionally included fraud, corruption, excess of authority and failure to accord procedural due process. On this matter would tax arbitration evolve in a similar or different direction from commercial arbitration? What ground (if any) should justify non-recognition of an award? What procedures (if any) should exist to permit explicit annulment of awards? And what existing treaties (such as the New York Convention) already applied to tax arbitration? He invited Professor Park to speak.

Professor Park said that lawyers had argued for decades about how to deal with procedural defects in commercial arbitration, such as an arbitrator's excess of authority. While arbitral awards should generally be final on the substantive merits of the dispute, awards would not usually be treated as 'binding' – regardless of what the arbitration agreement said – if the arbitrators exceeded the scope of jurisdiction conferred on them by the parties. All commercial arbitration treaties enumerated defects in procedural fairness that justified non-recognition of an arbitrator's findings. Several treaties also established binational panel procedures by which awards could be explicitly annulled even before presentation to a court. These non-recognition and annulment provisions were commonly called 'control mechanisms'. Similar control issues were bound to arise in tax arbitration. For example, arbitrators might have been asked to decide a transfer pricing dispute concerning royalties paid by a subsidiary to a parent and in determining the royalty rate the arbitrators might take into account transactions with a related company that one party considered to fall outside the scope of the arbitral agreement. (This happened in the recent Apple case, where a disagreement arose about whether transactions with a particular related company were to be considered in determining the income of the entity or entities covered by the arbitration). Another possibility was that the arbitrators might go on to express an opinion about arm's-length interest rates on inter-company loans. In such cases, courts might as a matter of public policy disregard the award as reaching beyond the arbitrator's jurisdiction. At present, tax treaties did not deal with grounds for non-recognition of awards. This silence left arbitrators without guidance on a number of basic questions (such as whether their awards must contain reasons) and left open the possibility that national courts would develop inconsistent standards for the recognition of awards. Designing control mechanisms for international tax arbitration raised three basic questions: (1) What grounds should justify non-recognition of an award? (2) What (if any) binational procedures should provide for explicit annulment or setting aside of an award? (3) What existing multilateral arbitration treaties already covered tax arbitration? In answer to the first question, most commercial arbitration treaties provided for the non-recognition of awards based on arbitrator bias, excess of authority or denial of one party's ability to present its case. Some arbitral systems went further and permitted annulment or non-recognition of an award that violated the forum's 'public policy' or required that the award state the reasons on which the decision was based. The optimum arbitration control mechanism should balance the competing goals of finality and fairness, weighing the legitimate interests of both the winners and the losers. It seemed best that non-recognition to tax treaty awards should be limited to three grounds: (a) arbitrator bias or corruption; (b) arbitrator excess of authority; (c) denial of one side's right to present its case. On balance, it was probably better not to deny recognition to tax awards on grounds of public policy. In answer to the second question, once treaty partners had reached a consensus on grounds for non-recognition, they needed to ask whether there should be a binational procedure for annulment of defective awards, along the lines of annulment procedures in the rules of the World Bank's International Center for the Settlement of Investment Disputes (ICSID). In answer to the third question, tax arbitration was now covered by the 1958 New York Arbitration Convention. The New York Convention required recognition of arbitral awards in ninety countries, but subject to certain exceptions. Courts could refuse recognition to awards on grounds provided under Convention Article V. Most of these grounds related to procedural fairness and were non-controversial. However Article V(2)(b) of the Convention permitted non-recognition of awards that violated the malleable catch-all term 'Public policy'. This could be dangerous to the finality of tax arbitration, since fiscal matters by their nature usually implicated a forum's public policy. Professor Park believed that the New York Convention already covered international tax arbitration. The Convention explicitly gave contracting states the option to restrict its coverage to arbitrations 'arising out of legal relationships considered as commercial'. Many countries, including France, had decided not to limit the Convention to commercial disputes. Even in countries that had opted for the commercial limitation, such as the United States, transfer pricing disputes arguably did 'arise out of' a commercial relationship. The Iranian Claims arbitrations in The Hague represented an arbitral régime analogues to tax treaty arbitrations, in the sense that both systems were established by an inter-state treaty rather than the agreement of private individuals. The United States courts had held that Iranian Claims awards fell within the scope of the New York Convention. The Second Circuit had expressly refused to enforce an Iranian Claims award where the arbitrator failed to give one party an adequate opportunity to present its case and thus ran foul of Article 5 of the New York Convention. He ended by contrasting domestic and international tax arbitration. Domestic tax arbitration was like commercial arbitration in that the altenative was a national court proceeding. By contrast, for inter-state disputes under tax treaties, there was no binding alternative to arbitration, since there were no neutral courts with compulsory jurisdiction over the two states. Consequently, interstate arbitration awards deserved more deference than domestic tax (or commercial) awards and should be subject to fewer grounds on which the award might be set aside.

Professor Lindencrona opened a general discussion of topics four and five of section (II), and the following points were made:

1. Only an international court could handle a challenge to an international arbitral award. This meant the International Court of Justice at The Hague.
2. Tax treaties had a dual status, since they concerned both relations between states (public international law) and relations between state and taxpayer (domestic law). For example, two competent authorities might agree that in a particular case state A had the taxing right and the taxpayer might challenge this agreement on grounds of international law.

Professor Lindencrona opened the discussion of topic six of section (II): source of law. The principal source of law in an arbitration procedure was, of course, the double taxation convention. It was for consideration, however, whether other sources could be used as well, for example the Commentary to the OECD Model Convention or general principles of international tax law and previous awards. Even more important was the question to what extent the arbitrators could use the national tax law of the treaty-making states in interpreting the treaty. He invited Dr. Burckhardt to speak.

Dr. Burckhardt said that the source of law must be international treaties including arbitration treaties. It could not be national laws, except perhaps where the laws of both the states concerned coincided on a particular point. He gave five reasons why national laws were precluded from use in the procedure of international arbitration. First, once states had resorted to international arbitration it was no longer reasonable for them to invoke their national laws. Second, if national laws could be used by the arbitrators, this would give them something approaching powers of treaty override. Third, since any question outside the treaty was for that reason outside the jurisdiction of the arbitrators, the non-applicability of national laws raised no constitutional problems. Fourt, the non-applicability of national laws held good even for legislation providing for treaty override. Fifth, as a practical consideration, if national laws could be applied, worldwide consistency between arbitral awards would be unobtainable and multinationals would face different tax régimes for transfer pricing (for example) in the various countries where they operated. The Commentaries to the OECD Model Convention could be invoked where the countries concerned had entered no reservations: but the internal papers of the OECD were inadmissible. It was desirable that the arbitrator should enjoy a certain freedom of action, acting as some kind of *amiable compositeur* and applying some kind of *les mercatoria*; but they must stay within the ambit of the treaty.

Professor Hinnekens said that he agreed in general with Dr. Burkhardt. He formulated nine rules or principles concerning the source of substantive law applicable under the European Community Arbitration Convention. First, the Convention was governed in the first place by its text as the authentic expression of the intention of the parties. Second, the principles might be defined in Article 4; but further definition and clarification were required. The OECD Commentaries and Reports on transfer pricing and multinational enterprises were therefore a useful international source of interpretation. Third, as an exception to the foregoing rule, the provisions of Paragraphs 7(i)(iii)(iv)(v) of the OECD Model were not to be found in the EC Convention. There were thus inconsistencies between the EC and the OECD in such matters as formula apportionments. Fourth, a decision based on equity or on considerations of practicability was not a decision based on arm's-length dealing and as such invalid on grounds of action in excess of the arbitrators' authority. Fifth, the rules of general international law and of the Vienna Convention on the Law of Treaties applied to the interpretation of the EC Arbitration Convention. Sixth, earlier arbitral awards were not binding on the parties in other procedures. Seventh, the national statutes, regulations and case law were, by their unilateral nature and resulting divergence, not a good source of law and interpretation for multilateral tax treaties (still less so than for bilateral tax treaties). However, an express referral to domestic tax law was found in the arbitration clause of some bilateral treaties (for example those of Germany). The general interpretation rule of the EC Convention referred to the general interpretation rule of the bilateral agreements between the Member States, which in turn referred to the *lex fori* as long as the context and the purpose of the treaty were satisfied. Eight, domestic law would become a better source if it were harmonised at the EC level. Ninth, EC harmonisation and arbitration were likely to produce spill-over effects on the interpretation of the same tax provisions in states which were not members of the Community and for that reason not party to the Convention.

Professor Lindencrona opened the discussion of topic seven of section (II), the scope of the arbitration award. Should it be limited to the interpretation and application of the treaty or should it also take account of the relationship between the treaty and national tax law and thus almost decide the amount of tax the taxpayer should pay? In the latter case, which national laws? Should the award be limited to questions of law or could questions of fact be involved as well (as, for example, finding an arm's-length price in a transfer-pricing case)? He invited Professor Burgio to speak.

Professor Burgio said that at the bilateral level the scope of the arbitration award depended on the terms of reference. Under the EC Convention, Article

4 was binding. The Convention covered sixty-six possible bilateral relationships between Member States, and of these sixty-six relationships fifty-seven had treaties in force. The nine missing treaties created problems in starting the procedure. He added that the reference to other treaties in Article 15 of the EC Convention was indirectly a reference to domestic law.

Professor Lindencrona introduced the discussion of section (III): future development. Was it desirable that arbitration clauses should be introduced into more treaties? Should these clauses be different from the existing ones? What was the final goal – a network of arbitration clauses or one (or several) international tax courts? He invited Dr. Burckhardt to speak.

Dr. Burckhardt said that there were many supporters of arbitration, including the Business and Industry Advisory Committee to the OECD (BIAC), the International Chamber of Commerce (ICC) and the International Fiscal Association. A realistic assessment was required. The taxpayer wanted, not arbitration as such, but removal of double taxation. What did the taxpayer require of arbitration? His international tax problems should be solved quickly, competently, with international consistency, reliably over a period of time, by a truly independent body having the required experience in law and in fact, with full confidentiality and fully eliminating double taxation. He gave four reasons why it would be unwise to trade in the mutual agreement procedure for the uncertain advantages of arbitration. First, although a mutual agreement procedure did not invariably procedure a result, this outcome was rare or very rare. Second, although the results of the mutual agreement procedure might seem to be based on horse-trading, the same could be said of arbitration. Third, although the procedural rights of the taxpayer might in theory be enhanced by arbitration, in practice this improvement was only marginal. Moreover, the process of arbitration was generally lengthier than that of the mutual agreement procedure, and the taxpayer might prefer a less favourable decision provided he could obtain it earlier. Finally under this heading, confidentiality was more secure under the mutual agreement procedure than it was under arbitration. Fourth, because of the wide differences between commercial and tax arbitration, the success of the former could not be used as an agreement for the latter.

Professor Ritter said that Dr. Burckhardt had dealt with a number of important points concerning cases that could be settled under the mutual agreement procedure. But what about the difficult cases? He presented seven theses in favour of an independent arbitration procedure in international tax conflicts. First, the struggle for revenue between states was increasing instead of decreasing. Second, within this scenario the danger for the taxpayer was increasing and he was becoming an object of tax conflict between states. Third, this development contradicted the growing internationalisation of commerce. Fourth, the success of the mutual agreement procedure was dependent on the willingness of the states concerned to reach appropriate solutions. Fifth, the disappearance of the taxpayer's protection could be avoided only by giving him the right, in case of the failure of the mutual agreement procedure, to require a decision from an independent tribunal which was also binding on the states concerned. Sixth, the stubborn resistance of many states to such independent arbitration was indefensible. Seventh, a mandatory arbitration procedure depending on the taxpayer for its initiation would compel the states to draw their legal positions together rather than letting them drift apart.

Professor Burgio spoke of the European Commission's serious concern about its responsibility to ensure that the single market functioned effectively. The EC Convention was designed to tackle the increase in the number of cases of double taxation. Some of its rules might not be observed, and they would in any case be void if the Convention was not ratified; five Member States had not ratified so far.

The discussion was opened to the floor and the following were the principal points made:

1. The competent authorities would be less, not more, willing to compromise under arbitration than under the mutual agreement procedure.
2. The mutual agreement procedure had the advantage of being voluntary rather than mandatory. It was helpful to federal states and served to improve relationships between taxpayers and tax administrations.
3. Some areas of tax policy might be matters of principle to governments, which would not be willing to yield the last word to an international tribunal.

Summing up, Professor Lindencrona said that despite the criticisms voiced at the Seminar he still considered arbitration a big step forward. A speaker had pointed to the presence of arbitration articles in existing treaties. Arbitration was a subject to which IFA could return. He thanked the speakers and closed the Seminar.

CONVENTION[1]

On the elimination of double taxation in connection with the adjustment of profits of associated enterprises.

(90/436/EEC)

THE HIGH CONTRACTING PARTIES TO THE TREATY ESTABLISHING THE EUROPEAN ECONOMIC COMMUNITY

DESIRING to give effect to Article 220 of that Treaty, by virtue of which they have undertaken to enter into negotiations with one another with a view to securing for the benefit of their nationals the elimination of double taxation.

CONSIDERING the importance attachted to the elimination of double taxation in connection with the adjustments of profits of associated enterprises.

HAVE DECIDED to conclude this Convention, and to this end have designated as their Plenipotentiaries:

HIS MAJESTY THE KING OF THE BELGIANS:

Philippe de SCHOUTHEETE de TERVARENT,
Ambassador Extraordinary and Plenipotentiary;

HER MAJESTY THE QUEEN OF DENMARK:

Niels HELVEG PETERSEN
Minister for Economic Affairs;

1. OJ No. L 225, 20 August 1990, p. 10.

THE PRESIDENT OF THE FEDERAL REPUBLIC OF GERMANY

Theo WAIGEL,
Federal Minister for Finance;
Jürgen TRUMPF,
Ambassador Extraordinary and Plenipotentiary;

THE PRESIDENT OF THE HELLENIC REPUBLIC:

Ioannis PALAIOKRASSAS,
Minister for Finance;

HIS MAJESTY THE KING OF SPAIN:

Carlos SOLCHAGA CATALÁN,
Minister for Economic Affairs and Finance;

THE PRESIDENT OF THE FRENCH REPUBLIC:

Jean VIDAL
Ambassador Extraordinary and Plenipotentiary;

THE PRESIDENT OF IRELAND:

Albert REYNOLDS,
Minister for Finance;

THE PRESIDENT OF THE ITALIAN REPUBLIC:

Stefano DE LUCA,
State Secretary for Finance;

HIS ROYAL HIGHNESS THE GRAND DUKE OF LUXEMBOURG:

Jean-Claude JUNCKER,
Minister for the Budget, Minister for Finance, Minister for Labour;

HER MAJESTY THE QUEEN OF THE NETHERLANDS:

P.C. NIEMAN,
Ambassador Extraordinary and Plenipotentiary;

THE PRESIDENT OF THE PORTUGUESE REPUBLIC:

Miguel BELEZA,
Minister for Finance;

HER MAJESTY THE QUEEN OF THE UNITED KINGDOM OF GREAT BRITAIN AND NORTHERN IRELAND:

David H.A. Hannay KCMG,
Ambassador Extraordinary and Plenipotentiary,

WHO, meeting within the Council and having exchanged their Full Powers, found in good and due form,

HAVE AGREED AS FOLLOWS:

Chapter I. Scope of the Convention

Article 1

1. This Convention shall apply where, for the purposes of taxation, profits which are included in the profits of an enterprise of a Contracting State are also included or are also likely to be included in the profits of an enterprise of another Contracting State on the grounds that the principles set out in Article 4 and applied either directly or in corresponding provisions of the law of the State concerned have not been observed.

2. For the purposes of this Convention, the permanent establishment of an enterprise of a Contracting State situated in another Contracting State shall be deemed to be an enterprise of the State in which it is situated.

3. Paragraph I shall also apply where any of the enterprises concerned have made losses rather than profits.

Article 2

1. This Convention shall apply to taxes on income.

2. The existing taxes to which this Convention shall apply are, in particular the following:

(a) in Belgium:
- impôt des personnes physiques/personenbelasting,
- impôt des sociétés/vennootschapsbelasting,
- impôt des personnes morales/rechtspersonenbelasting,
- impôt des non résidents/belasting der niet-verblijfhouders,
- taxe communale et taxe d'agglomération additionnelles à l'impôt des per-

sonnes physiques/aanvullende gemeentebelasting en agglomeratiebelasting op de personenbelasting;
(b) in Denmark:
- selskabsskat,
- indkomstskat til staten,
- kommunal indkomstskat,
- amtskommunal indkomstskat,
- særlig indkomstskat,
- kirkeskat,
- udbytteskat,
- renteskat,
- royaltyskat,
- frigørelsesafgift;
(c) in the Federal Republic of Germany:
- Einkommensteuer,
- Körperschaftssteuer,
- Gewerbesteuer, in so far as this tax is based on trading profits;
(d) in Greece:
- phoros eisodematos fusikon prosopon,
- phoros eisodematos nomikon prosopon,
- esifora uper ton epicheireseon udreuses kai apocheteuses;
(e) in Spain:
- impuesto sobre la renta de las personas físicas,
- impuesto sobre sociedades;
(f) in France:
- impôt sur le revenu,
- impôt sur les sociétés;
(g) in Ireland:
- Income Tax,
- Corporation Tax;
(h) in Italy:
- imposta sul reddito delle persone fisiche,
- imposta sul reddito delle persone giuridiche,
- imposta locale sui redditi;
(i) in Luxembourg:
- impôt sur le revenu des personnes physiques,
- impôt sur le revenu des collectivités,
- impôt commercial, in so far as this tax is based on trading profits;
(j) in the Netherlands:
- inkomstenbelasting,
- vennootschapsbelasting;
(k) in Portugal:
- imposto sobre o rendomento das pessoas singulares,

- imposto sobre o rendimento das pessoas colectivas,
- derrama para os municípios sobre o imposto sobre o rendimento da pessoas colectivas;

(l) in the United Kingdom:
- Income Tax,
- Corporation Tax,

3. The Convention shall also apply to any identical or similar taxes which are imposed after the date of signature thereof in addition to, or in place of existing taxes. The competent authorities of the Contracting States shall inform each other of any changes made in the respective domestic laws.

Chapter II. General Provisions

Section I. Definitions

Article 3

1. For the purposes of this Convention: 'competent authority' shall mean:

- in Belgium:
  De Minister van Financiën or an authorized representative,
  Le Ministre des Finances or an authorized representative,
- in Denmark:
  Skattenministeren or an authorized representative,
- in the Federal Republic of Germany:
  Der Bundesminister der Finanzen or an authorized representative,
- in Greece:
  O Upourgos, ton Oihonomikon or an authorized representative,
- in Spain:
  El Ministro de Economía y Hacienda or an authorized representative,
- in France:
  Le Ministre chargé du budget or an authorized representative,
- in Ireland:
  The Revenue Commissioners or an authorized representative,
- in Italy:
  Il Ministro della Finanze or an authorized representative,
- in Luxembourg:
  Le Ministre des Finances or an authorized representative,
- in the Netherlands:
  De Minister van Financiën or an authorized representative,
- in Portugal:
  O Ministro das Finanças or an authorized representative,
- in the United Kingdom:
  The Commissioners of Inland Revenue or an authorized representative.

2. Any term not defined in this Convention shall, unless the context otherwise requires, have the meaning which it has under the double taxation convention between the States concerned.

Section II. Principles applying to the Adjustment of Profits of Associated Enterprises and to the Attribution of Profits to Permanent Establishments

Article 4

The following principles shall be observed in the application of this Convention:

1. Where:

(a) an enterprise of a Contracting State participates directly or indirectly in the management, control or capital of an enterprise of another Contracting State, or

(b) the same persons participate directly or indirectly in the management, control or capital of an enterprise of one Contracting State and an enterprise of another Contracting State,

and in either case conditions are made or imposed between the two enterprises in their commercial or financial relations which differ from those which would be made between independent enterprises, then any profits which would, but for those conditions, have accrued to one of the enterprises, but, by reason of those conditions, have not so accrued, may be included in the profits of that enterprise and taxed accordingly.

2. Where an enterprise of a Contracting State carries on business in another Contracting State through a permanent establishment situated therein, there shall be attributed to that permanent establishment the profits which it might be expected to make if it were a distinct and separate enterprise engaged in the same or similar activities under the same or similar conditions and dealing wholly independently with the enterprise of which it is a permanent establishment.

Article 5

Where a Contracting State intends to adjust the profits of an enterprise in accordance with the principles set out in Article 4, it shall inform the enterprise of the intended action in due time and give it the opportunity to inform the other enterprise so as to give that other enterprise the opportunity to inform in turn the other Contracting State.

However, the Contracting State providing such information shall not be prevented from making the proposed adjustment.

If after such information has been given the two enterprises and the other Contracting State agree to the adjustment, Articles 6 and 7 shall not apply.

Section III. Mutual agreement and Arbitration Procedure

Article 6

1. Where an enterprise considers that, in any case to which this Convention applies, the principles set out in Article 4 have not been observed, it may, irrespective of the remedies provided by the domestic law of the Contracting States concerned, present its case to the competent authority of the Contracting State of which it is an enterprise or in which its permanent establishment is situated. The case must be presented within three years of the first notification of the action which results or is likely to result in double taxation within the meaning of Article 1.

The enterprise shall at the same time notify the competent authority if other Contracting States may be concerned in the case. The competent authority shall then without delay notify the competent authorities of those other Contracting States.

2. If the complaint appears to it to be well-founded and if it is not itself able to arrive at a satisfactory solution, the competent authority shall endeavour to resolve the case by mutual agreement with the competent authority of any other Contracting State concerned, with a view to the elimination of double taxation on the basis of the principles set out in Article 4. Any mutual agreement reached shall be implemented irrespective of any time limits prescribed by the domestic laws of the Contracting States concerned.

Article 7

1. If the competent authorities concerned fail to reach an agreement that eliminates the double taxation referred to in Article 6 within two years of the date on which the case was first submitted to one of the competent authorities in accordance with Article 6(1), they shall set up an advisory commission charged with delivering its opinion on the elimination of the double taxation in question.

Enterprises may have recourse to the remedies available to them under the domestic law of the Contracting States concerned; however, where the case has so been submitted to a court or tribunal, the term of two years referred to in the first subparagraph shall be computed from the date on which the judgment of the final court of appeal was given.

2. The submission of the case to the advisory commission shall not prevent a Contracting State from initiating or continuing judicial proceedings or proceedings for administrative penalties in relation to the same matters.

3. Where the domestic law of a Contracting State does not permit the competent authorities of that State to derogate from the decision of their judicial bodies, paragraph 1 shall not apply unless the associated enterprise of that State has allowed the time provided for appeal to expire, or has withdrawn any such appeal before a decision has been delivered. This provision shall not affect the ap-

peal if and in so far as it relates to matters other than those referred to in Article 6.

4. The competent authorities may by mutual agreement and with the agreement of the associated enterprises concerned waive the time limits referred to in paragraph 1.

5. In so far as the provisions of paragraphs 1 to 4 are not applied, the rights of each of the associated enterprises, as laid down in Article 6, shall be unaffected.

Article 8

1. The competent authority of a Contracting State shall not be obliged to initiate the mutual agreement procedure or to set up the advisory commission referred to in Article 7 where legal or administrative proceedings have resulted in a final ruling that by actions giving rise to an adjustment of transfers of profits under Article 4 one of the enterprises concerned is liable to a serious penalty.

2. Where judicial or administrative proceedings, initiated with a view to a ruling that by actions giving rise to an adjustment of profits under Article 4 one of the enterprises concerned was liable to a serious penalty, are being conducted simultaneously with any of the proceedings referred to in Articles 6 and 7, the competent authorities may stay the latter proceedings until the judicial or administrative proceedings have been concluded.

Article 9

1. The advisory commission referred to in Article 7(1) shall consist of, in addition to its Chairman:

- two representative of each competent authority concerned; this number may be reduced to one by agreement between the competent authorities,
- an even number of independent persons of standing to be appointed by mutual agreement from the list of persons referred to in paragraph 4 or, in the absence of agreement, by the drawing of lots by the competent authorities concerned.

2. When the independent persons of standing are appointed an alternate shall be appointed for each of them according to the rules for the appointment of the independent persons in case the independent persons are prevented from carrying out their duties.

3. Where lots are drawn, each of the competent authorities may object to the appointment of any particular independent person of standing in any circumstance agreed in advance between the competent authorities concerned or in one of the following situations:

- where that person belongs to or is working on behalf of one of the tax administrations concerned,
- where that person has, or has had, a large holding in or is or has been an employee of or adviser to one or each of the associated enterprises,

– where that person does not offer a sufficient guarantee of objectivity for the settlement of the case or cases to be decided.

4. The list of independent persons of standing shall consist of all the independent persons nominated by the Contracting States. For this purpose each Contracting State shall nominate five persons and shall inform the Secretary-General of the Council of the European Communities thereof.

Such persons must be nationals of a Contracting State and resident within the territory to which this Convention applies. They must be competent and independent.

The Contracting States may make alterations to the list referred to in the first subparagraph; they shall inform the Secretary-General of the Council of the European Communities thereof without delay.

5. The representatives and independent persons of standing appointed in accordance with paragraph 1 shall elect a Chairman from among those persons of standing on the list referred to in paragraph 4, without prejudice to the right of each competent authority concerned to object to the appointment of the person of standing thus chosen in one of the situations referred to in paragraph 3.

The Chairman must possess the qualifications required for appointment to the highest judicial offices in his country or be a jurisconsult of recognized competence.

6. The members of advisory commission shall keep secret all matters which they learn as a result of the proceedings. The Contracting States shall adopt appropriate provisions to penalize any breach of secrecy obligations. They shall, without delay inform the Commission of the European Communities of the measures taken. The Commission of the European Communities shall inform the other Contracting States.

7. The Contracting States shall take all necessary steps to ensure that the advisory commission meets without delay once cases are referred to it.

Article 10

1. For the purposes of the procedure referred to in Article 7, the associated enterprises concerned may provide any information, evidence or documents which seem to them likely to be of use to the advisory commission in reaching a decision. The enterprises and the competent authorities of the Contracting States concerned shall give effect to any request made by de advisory commission to provide information, evidence or documents. However, the competent authorities of any such Contracting State shall not be under any obligation:

(a) to carry out administrative measures at variance with its domestic law or its normal administrative practice;
(b) to supply information which is not obtainable under its domestic law or in its normal administrative practice; or
(c) to supply information which would disclose any trade, business, industrial

or professional secret or trade process, or information the disclosure of which would be contrary to public policy (ordre public).

2. Each of the associated enterprises may, at its request, appear or be represented before the advisory commission. If the advisory commission so requests, each of the associated enterprises shall appear or be represented before it.

Article 11

The advisory commission referred to in Article 7 shall deliver its opinion not more than six months from the date on which the matter was referred to it.

The advisory commission must base its opinion on Article 4.

2. The advisory commission shall adopt its opinion by a simple majority of its members. The competent authorities concerned may agree on additional rules or procedure.

3. The costs of the advisory commission procedure, other than those incurred by the associated enterprises, shall be shared equally by the Contracting States concerned.

Article 12

1. The competent authorities party to the procedure referred to in Article 7 shall, acting by common consent on the basis of Article 4, take a decision which will eliminate the double taxation within six months of the date on which the advisory commission delivered its opinion.

The competent authorities may take a decision which deviated from the advisory commission's opinion. If they fail to reach agreement, they shall be obliged to act in accordance with that opinion.

2. The competent authorities may agree to publish the decision referred to in paragraph 1, subject to the consent of the enterprises concerned.

Article 13

The fact that the decisions taken by the Contracting States, concerning the taxation of profits resulting from a transaction between associated enterprises, have become final shall not prevent recourse to the procedures set out in Articles 6 and 7.

Article 14

For the purposes of this Convention, the double taxation of profits shall be regarded as eliminated if either:

(a) the profits are included in the computation of taxable profits in one State only; or

(b) the tax chargeable on those profits in one State is reduced by an amount equal to the tax chargeable on them in the other.

Chapter III. Final Provisions

Article 15

Nothing in this Convention shall affect the fulfilment of wider obligations with respect to the elimination of double taxation in the case of an adjustment of profits of associated enterprises resulting either from other conventions to which the Contracting States are or will become parties or from the domestic law of the Contracting States.

Article 16

1. The territorial scope of this Convention shall be that defined in Article 227(1) of the Treaty establishing the European Economic Community, without prejudice to paragraph 2 of this Article.

2. This Convention shall not apply to:
- the French territories referred to in Annex IV to the Treaty establishing the European Economic Community,
- the Faroe Islands and Greenland.

Article 17

This Convention will be ratified by the Contracting States. The instruments of ratification will be deposited at the office of the Secretary-General of the Council of the European Communities.

Article 18

This Convention shall enter into force on the first day of the third month following that in which the instrument of ratification is deposited by the last signatory State to take that step. The Convention shall apply to proceedings referred to in Article 6(1) which are initiated after its entry into force.

Article 19

The Secretary-General of the Council of the European Communities shall inform the Contracting States of:
(a) the deposit of each instrument of ratification;
(b) the date on which this Convention will enter into force;
(c) the list of independent persons of standing appointed by the Contracting States and any alterations thereto in accordance with Article 9(4).

Article 20

This Convention is concluded for a period of five years. Six months before the expiry of that period, the Contracting States will meet to decide on the extension of this Convention and any other relevant measure.

Article 21

Each Contracting State may, at any time, ask for a revision of this Convention. In that event, a conference to revise the Convention will be convened by the President of the Council of the European Communities.

Article 22

This Convention, drawn up in a single original in the Danish, Dutch, English, French, German, Greek, Irish, Italian, Portuguese and Spanish languages, all 10 texts being equally authentic, shall be deposited in the archives of the General Secretariat of the Council of the European Communities. The Secretary-General shall transmit a certified copy to the Government of each Signatory State.

Final Act

The plenipotentiaries of the high contracting parties.

meeting at Brussels, on the twenty-third day of July nineteenhundred and ninety, for the signature of the Convention on the elimination of double taxation in connection with the adjustment of profits of associated enterprises.

have, on the occasion of signing the said Convention:

(a) adopted the following joint Declarations attached to the Final Act:
   - Declaration on Article 4(1),
   - Declaration on Article 9(6),
   - Declaration on Article 13;

(b) taken note of the following unilateral Declarations attached to this Final Act:
   - Declaration of France and the United Kingdom on Article 7,
   - Individual Declarations of the Contracting States on Article 8,
   - Declaration of the Federal Republic of Germany on Article 16.

In witness whereof, the undersigned have signed this Final Act.

Done at Brussels on the twenty-third day of July in the year one thousand nine hundred and ninety.

Joint Declaration

Declaration on Article 4(1)

The provisions of Article 4(1) shall cover both cases where a transaction is carried out directly between two legally distinct enterprises as well as cases where a transaction is carried out between one of the enterprises and the permanent establishment of the other enterprise situated in a third country.

Declaration on Article 9(6)

The Member States shall be entirely free as regards the nature and scope of the appropriate provisions they adopt for penalizing any breach of secrecy obligations.

Declarations on Article 13

Where, in one or more of the Contracting States concerned, the decisions regarding the taxation giving rise to the procedures referred to in Articles 6 and 7 have been altered after the procedure referred to in Article 6 has been concluded or after the decision referred to in Article 12 has been taken and where double taxation within the meaning of Article 1 results, account being taken of the application of the outcome of that procedure or that decision, Articles 6 and 7 shall apply.

Unilateral Declarations

Declaration on Article 7

France and the United Kingdom declare that they will apply Article 7(3).

Individual Declarations of the Contracting States on Article 8

Belgium

The term 'serious penalty' means a criminal or administrative penalty in cases:
- either of a common law offence committed with the aim of tax evasion,
- or infringements of the provisions of the Code of income tax or of decisions taken in implementation thereof, committed with fraudulent intention or with the intention of causing injury.

Denmark

The concept of 'serious penalty' means a penalty for the intentional infringement of provisions of the Criminal Law or of special legislation in cases which cannot be regulated by administrative means.

Cases of infringement of provisions of tax law may, as a general rule, be regulated by administrative means where it is considered that the infringement will not entail a punishment greater than a fine.

Germany

An infringement of the tax laws punishable by a 'serious penalty' is constituted by any infringement of the tax laws penalized by detention, criminal or administrative fines.

Greece

Under Greek legislation governing taxation, an undertaking is liable to 'severe penalties':

1. if it fails to submit declarations, or submits incorrect declarations, in respect of taxes, charges or contributions which must be withheld and paid to the State under existing provisions, or in respect of value added tax, turnover tax or the special tax on luxury goods, in so far as the total amount of the above taxes, charges and contributions which should have been declared and paid to the State as a result of trade or other activities carried out over a period of six months exceeds an amount of six hundred thousand (600,000) Greek drachmas or one million (1,000,000) Greek drachmas over a period of one calendar year;
2. if it fails to submit a declaration of income tax, in so far as the tax due in respect of the income not declared is more than three hundred thousand (300,000) Greek drachmas;
3. if it fails to supply the taxation details laid down in the Code on Taxation Data;
4. if it supplies details as referred to under the previous case 3, which are incorrect as regards quantity or unit price or value, in so far as the inaccuracy results in a discrepancy which exceeds ten per cent (10%) of the total amount or of the total value of the goods, the provision of services or the trade generally;
5. if it fails to keep accurately the books and records required by the Code on Taxation Data, in so far as that inaccuracy has been noted in the course of a regular check, the findings of which have been confirmed either by administrative resolution of the discrepancy or because the period allowed for an appeal has expired or as a result of a definitive decision by an administrative tribunal, provided that during the management period checked the discrepancy between gross income and the income declared is more than twenty per cent (20%) and in any case not less than one million (1,000,000) Greek drachmas;
6. if it fails to observe the obligation to keep books and records as laid down in the relevant provisions of the Code on Taxation Data;
7. if it issues false or fictitious – or itself falsifies – invoices for the sale of goods or the supply of services or any taxation details as referred to in case 3 above.

A taxation document is regarded as false if it has been perforated or stamped in any way without the proper authentication having been entered in the relevant books of the competent tax authority, in so far as failure to make such an entry has occurred in the knowledge that such authentication is required for the taxation document. A taxation document is also regarded as false if the content and other details of the original or the copy differ from those which are recorded on the counterfoil of that document.
A taxation document is regarded as fictitious if it has been issued for a transaction or part of a transaction, transfer or any other reasons not recorded in the total or for a transaction carried out by persons different from those recorded in the taxation document;

8. if it is aware of the intention of the action taken and collaborates in any way in the production of false taxation documents or is aware that the documents are false or fictitious and collaborates in any way in their issue or accepts the false, fictitious or falsified taxation documents with the intention of concealing material relevant to taxation.

Spain

The term 'serious penalites' includes administrative penalties for serious tax infringements, as well as criminal penalties for offences committed with respect to the taxation authorities.

France

The term 'serious penalties' includes criminal penalties and tax penalties such as penalties for failure to make a tax return after receiving a summons, for lack of good faith, for fraudulent practices, for opposition to tax inspection, for secret payments or distribution, or far abuse of rights.

Ireland

'Serious penalties' shall include penalties for:
(a) failing to make a return;
(b) fraudulently or negligently making an incorrect return;
(c) failing to keep proper records;
(d) failing to make documents and records available for inspection;
(e) obstructing persons exercising statutory powers;
(f) failing to notify chargeability to tax;
(g) making a false statement to obtain an allowance.

The legislative provisions governing these offences, as at 3 July 1990, are as follows:
- Part XXXV of the Income Tax Act, 1967,

- Section 6 of the Finance Act, 1968,
- Part XIV of the Corporation Tax Act, 1976,
- Section 94 of the Finance Act, 1983.

Any subsequent provisions replacing, amending or updating the penalty code would also be comprehended.

Italy

The term 'serious penalties' means penalties laid down for illicit acts, within the meaning of the domestic law, constituting a tax offence.

Luxembourg

Luxembourg considers to be a 'serious penalty' what the other Contracting State considers to be so for the purposes of Article 8.

Netherlands

The term 'serious penalty' means a penalty imposed by a judge for any action, committed intentionally, which is mentioned in Article 68 of the General Law on taxation.

Portugal

The term 'serious penalties' includes criminal penalties as well as the further tax penalties applicable to infringements committed with intent to defraud or in which the fine applicable is of an amount exceeding 1,000,000 (one million) Portugese escudos.

United Kingdom

The United Kingdom will interpret the term 'serious penalty' as comprising criminal sanctions and administrative sanctions in respect of the fraudulent or negligent delivery of incorrect accounts, claims or returns for tax purposes.

Declaration by the Federal Republic of Germany on Article 16

The Government of the Federal Republic of Germany reserves the right to declare, when lodging its instrument of ratification that the Convention also applies to Land of Berlin.

The German-Swedish Tax Treaty (Unofficial Translation)

Article 44 (5)

Regarding the solution of conflicts under International Law resulting from this Convention, the European Convention as of 29 April 1957 for the Peaceful Settlement of Disputes does apply. The Contracting States may agree, however, instead of the procedure stipulated therein upon a Court of Arbitration, whose decision will be binding for the Contracting States. This Court shall consist of judges of the courts of the Contracting States or of third countries or of international organizations. Its procedure will be in accordance with internationally recognized principles of arbitration procedures. The parties concerned shall have the right to completely present their case and propose their own motions. The decision will be based upon the treaties of the Contracting States and the general international law; a decision *ex aequo et bono* is inadmissible. Until the time it has been agreed upon the invocation and the formation of the Court of Arbitration as well as upon its procedure, each Contracting State may proceed under Sentence 1.'

The German-French tax treaty. Amending protocol of 28 september 1989 to the convention of 29 July 1959 between the Federal Republic of Germany and the French Republic for the avoidance of double taxation and the establishment of rules for reciprocal administrative and legal assistance with respect to taxes on income and capital, business tax and land tax, as amended by the amending protocol of 9 Juni 1969 (unofficial translation)

Article 7

After Article 25 of the Convention 25a shall be inserted with the following wording:

> *'Article 25A*
>
> 1. With respect to cases referred to in Article 25, the competent authorities may decide to appoint an Arbitration Commission if they cannot reach an agreement within a period of 24 months from the day the taxpayer has presented his case.
>
> 2. This Arbitration Commission shall, for each single case, be established as follows: Each of the Contracting States appoints a representative; both representatives appoint, by mutual agreement, a delegate of a third state who is appointed chairman. All representative must be appointed within three months from the day the competent authorities have agreed to present the case to the Arbitration Commission.
>
> 3. Where the time limits referred to in paragraph 2 are not observed and no other arrangement is made, each of the Contracting States may call upon the

Secretary General of the Permanent Court of Arbitration to implement the necessary appointments.
4. The Arbitration Commission shall resolve the disagreement in accordance with the rules of international law and, especially, with the provisions of this Convention. It shall establish the mode of operation itself. The taxpayer shall be entitled to a hearing before the Commission or to present his applications in writing.
5. The decisions shall be made by the Commission with a majority of votes; they shall be binding. The absence of, or abstention from vote by, one of the States' representatives shall not impede the commission in making a decision. In case of a tie, the chairman's vote is decisive.'

US-German Tax Treaty 29 August 1994

Article 25 (5)
'Disagreement between the Contracting States regarding the interpretation or application of this Convention shall, as far as possible, be settled by the competent authorities. If a disagreement cannot be resolved by the competent authorities it may, if both authorities agree, be submitted for arbitration. The procedure shall be agreed upon and shall be established between the Contracting States by notes to be exchanged through diplomatic channels.'

Protocol

Paragraph 23
'With reference to paragraph 5 of Article 25
(Mutual Agreement Procedure)
The decision of the arbitration board in a particular case shall be binding on both Contracting States with respect to that case.'

Exchange of Letters

EMBASSY OF THE UNITED STATES OF AMERICA

Bonn 29 August 1989

Excellency,

I have the honor to confirm receipt of your Note of today's date which reads as follows:

'I have the honor to refer to the Convention signed today between the Federal Republic of Germany and the United States of America for the Avoidance of Double Taxation and the Prevention of Fiscal Evasion with respect to Taxes on Income and Capital and to certain other Taxes and to inform you on behalf of the Government of the Federal Republic of Germany of the following:

If the competent authorities of both Contracting States agree to submit a disagreement regarding the interpretation or application of this Convention to arbitration according to paragraph 5 of Article 25, the following procedures will apply:

1. The competent authorities may agree to invoke arbitration in a specific case only after fully exhausting the procedures available under paragraphs 1 to 4 of Article 25, and if the taxpayer(s) consent(s) to the arbitration and agree(s) in writing to be bound by the arbitration decision. The competent authorities will not generally accede to arbitration with respect to matters concerning the tax policy or domestic tax law of either Contracting State.

2. The competent authorities shall establish an arbitration board for each specific case in the following manner:
(a) An arbitration board shall consist of not less than three members. Each competent authority shall appoint the same number of members, and these members shall agree on the appointment of the other member(s).
(b) The other member(s) of the arbitration board shall be from either Contracting State or from another OECD member country. The competent authorities may issue further instructions regarding the criteria for selecting the other member(s) of the arbitration board.
(c) Arbitration board members (and their staffs) upon their appointment must agree in writing to abide by and be subject to the applicable confidentiality and disclosure provisions of both Contracting States and the Convention. In case those provisions conflict, the most restrictive condition will apply.

3. The Competent authorities may agree on and instruct the arbitration board regarding specific rules of procedure, such as appointment of a chairman, procedures for reaching a decision, establishment of time limits, etc. Otherwise, the arbitration board shall establish its own rules of procedure consistent with generally accepted principles of equity.

4. Taypayer's and/or their representatives shall be afforded the opportunity to present their views to the arbitration board.

5. The arbitration board shall decide each specific case on the basis of the Convention, giving due consideration to the domestic laws of the Contracting States

and the principles of international law. The arbitration board will provide to the competent authorities an explanation of its decision. The decision of the arbitration board in a particular case shall be binding on both Contracting States and the taxpayer(s) with respect to that case. While the decision of the arbitration board shall not have precedential effect, it is expected that such decisions ordinarily will be taken into account in subsequent competent authority cases involving the same taxpayer(s), the same issue(s), and substantially similar facts, and may also be taken into account in other cases where appropriate.

6. Costs for the arbitration procedure will be borne in the following manner:
(a) Each Contracting State shall bear the cost of remuneration for the member(s) appointed by it, as well as for its representation in the proceedings before the arbitration board;
(b) the cost of remuneration for the other member(s) and all other costs of the arbitration board shall be shared equally between the Contracting States; and
(c) the arbitration board may decide on a different allocation of costs.

However, if it deems appropriate in a specific case, in view of the nature of the case and the roles of the parties, the Competent Authority of a Contracting State may require the taxpayer(s) to agree to bear that Contracting State's share of the costs as a prerequisite for arbitration.

7. The competent authorities may agree to modify or supplement these procedures; however, they shall continue to be bound by the general principles established herein.

If this proposal meets with the approval of the Government of the United States of America, this Note and your reply thereto shall constitute the agreement of our two governments on these matters.

I have the honor to inform you, that my Government agrees to the above.

Accept, Excellency, the expression of my highest consideration.

Vernon A. Walters

US-Dutch Treaty

Article 29(5)

'If any difficulty or doubt arising as to the interpretation or application of this Convention cannot be resolved by the competent authorities in a mutual agreement procedure pursuant to the previous paragraphs of this Article, the case may, if both competent authorities and the taxpayer(s) agree, be submitted for arbitration, provided that the taxpayer agrees in writing to be bound by the dicision of the arbitration board. The decision of the arbitration board in a particular case shall be binding on both states with respect to that case. The provisions of this paragraph shall have effect after the States have so agreed through the exchange of diplomatic notes.'

US-Mexican Treaty of 18 September 1992

Article 26(5)

'If any difficulty or doubt arising as to the interpretation or application of this Convention cannot be resolved by the competent authorities in a mutual agreement procedure pursuant to the previous paragraphs of this Article, the case may, if both competent authorities and the taxpayer(s) agree, be submitted for arbitration, provided that the taxpayer agrees in writing to be bound by the decision of the arbitration board. The decision of the arbitration board in a particular case shall be binding on both states with respect to that case. The procedures shall be established between the States by notes to be exchanged through diplomatic channels. The provisions of this paragraph shall have effect after the States have so agreed through the exchange of diplomatic notes.'

Protocol

18. With reference to paragraph 5 of Article 26 (Mutual Agreement Procedure)

(a) After a period of three years after the entry into force of this Convention, the competent authorities shall consult in order to determine whether it is appropriate to make the exchange of diplomatic notes referred to in paragraph 5 of Article 26 (Mutual Agreement Procedure).
(b) If the competent authorities of both States agree to submit a disagreement regarding the interpretation or application of this Convention is a specific case to arbitration according to paragraph 5 of Article 26, the following procedures will apply;
    (i) If, in applying paragraphs 1 to 4 of Article 26, the competent authorities fail to reach an agreement within two years of the date on which the case was submitted to one of the competent authorities, they may agree to invoke arbitration in a specific case, but only after fully exhausting the procedures available for paragraph 1 to 4 of Article 26. The competent authorities will not accede to arbitration with respect to matters concerning the tax policy or domestic law of either State.

(ii) The competent authorities shall establish an arbitration board for each specific case in the following manner:

A. An arbitration board shall consist of not fewer than three members. Each competent authority shall appoint the same number of members, and these members shall agree on the appointment of the other member(s). The competent authorities may issue further instructions regarding the criteria for selecting the other member(s) of the arbitration board.

B. Arbitration board member(s) (and their staffs) upon their appointment must agree in writing to abide by and be subject to the applicable confidentiality and disclosure provisions of both States and the Convention. In case those provisions conflict, the most restrictive condition will apply.

(iii) The competent authorities may agree on and instruct the arbitration board regarding specific rules of procedure, such as appointment of a chairman, procedures for reaching a decision, establishment of time limits, etc. Otherwise, the arbitration board shall establish its own rules of procedure consistent with generally accepted principles of equity.

(iv) Taxpayers and/or their representatives shall be afforded the opportunity to present their views to the arbitration board.

(v) The arbitration board shall decide each specific case on the basis of the Convention, giving due consideration to the domestic laws of the States and the principles of international law. The arbitration board will provide to the competent authorities an explanation of its decision. The decision of the arbitration board shall be binding on both States and the taxpayer(s) with respect to that case. While the decision of the Arbitration board shall not have precedential effect, it is expected that such decisions ordinarily will be taken into account in subsequent competent authority cases involving the same taxpayer(s), the same issue(s) and substantially similar facts, and may also be taken into account in other cases where appropriate.

(vi) Costs for the arbitration procedure will be borne in the following manner:

A. each state shall bear the cost of remuneration for the member(s) appointed by it, as well as for its representation in the proceedings before the arbitration board;

B. the cost of remuneration for the other member(s) and all other costs of the arbitration board shall be shared equally between the States; and

C. the arbitration board may decide on a different allocation of costs.

However, if it deems appropriate in a specific case, in view of the nature of the case and the roles of the parties, the competent authority of one of the States may require the taxpayer(s) to agree to bear that State's share of the costs as a prerequisite for arbitration.

(vii) The competent authorities may agree to modify or supplement these procedures; however, they shall continue to be bound by the general principles established herein.

INTERNATIONAL CHAMBER OF COMMERCE

The Resolution of International Tax Conflicts

The Commission on Taxation of the International Chamber of Commerce (Paris) prepared a document entitled 'The Resolution of International Tax Conflicts' (Doc. 180/240). The Resolution was submitted to and adopted by the International Chamber of Commerce (ICC) Council at its 146th Session in Stockholm on 16 June 1984.
The Resolution is reproduced below with the permission of the International Chamber of Commerce.

The Background

The development of trade and capital investments between the nations of the world depends to a large extent on feasible solutions to the problem of double taxation. The number of tax treaties has increased enormously during the last decades. This trend will continue as more and more treaties are entered into between developing countries and developed countries.

The growing fiscal needs of many states have also increased the danger of tax conflicts and resulting double taxation. Such double taxation must be avoided whether it occurs in its juridical form to a single taxpayer or in its economic form to more than one taxpayer.

The important and growing role of international tax law for a vast number of taxpayers in different countries, both individuals and corporations, has made it more urgent that international tax conflicts be resolved. It is a fact, however, that the present possible methods for resolving these conflicts are insufficient. The deficiencies and possible methods to overcome them are now beginning to be more widely discussed.

The question of resolving disputes in international tax cases has aroused interest, however, since the end of the 19th century. Even the very first double taxation conventions gave rise to the need of resolving cases which were not covered by the conventions. It was realized that the conventions were not sufficient to avoid or reduce double taxation. A procedure to resolve possible problems during the validity of the double taxation conventions was needed.

The period between the two World Wars is of interest since different methods of resolving disputes were used in the double taxation conventions concluded during that time. In some cases the conventions had rules for final decisions made by bodies beyond the control of the contracting States. Soon, however, other rules began to be included in the conventions which authorized the ministries of finance (the competent authorities) to enter into agreements in individual cases in which the intentions of the convention that double taxation should be avoided had not been fulfilled. Such rules began to be the usual ones.

The two methods did not, however, exclude one another. A procedure might start with negotiations between the competent authorities of the contracting States. If no settlement could be reached the procedure could be taken over by an impartial body.

Since the Second World War and particularly with the OECD model treaties the legal situation has become stabilized. Negotiations between the States through their competent authorities – the so-called mutual agreement procdure – has become the accepted method for the resolution of disputes under double taxation conventions.

The Mutual Agreement Procedure and Its Shortcomings

The mutual agreement procedure that has to a large extent been standardized by the work of the OECD and its model treaties of 1963 and 1977 may be said to have two basic functions in conventions for the avoidance of double taxation: (1) the improvement, refinement and further development of the convention and (2) a quasi-judicial procedure. It is the second function that is of interest for the resolution of international tax disputes. Its purpose is to arrive at an agreement between the contracting States which eliminates double taxation that is contrary to provisions of the convention as well as double taxation arising from other causes. This purpose is often fulfilled. There are, however, some defects in the present mutual agreement procedure, for which remedies must be found:

1. The most serious defect in the present system is that the mutual agreement procedure does not envisage a method for resolving a deadlock between two contracting States. The casuses of such a deadlock can vary. It could be supposed, however, that the most common one is the failure of the competent authorities in the two contracting States to agree on the interpretation of a relevant clause in the convention, so that they are unwilling to conclude an agreement eliminating the double taxation in question.
2. The position of the taxpayer is unsatisfactory. The taxpayer can appeal to the competent authority if he thinks that he has not been taxed according to the convention. The competent authority then decides if it is prepared to initiate the mutual agreement procedure. In some countries, but not in all, unilateral relief can be provided in the event that the mutual agreement procedure is not initiated. The taxpayer has no guarantee that the procedure will be initiated. If it is initiated, he has no guarantee that a decision will be reached.

In the event that a decision has been reached which was unfavorable to him, he might not even have an apportunity to rebut arguments which were adverse to him. He is not formally a party to the procedure which is entirely a matter between two States (or tax administrations). Certainly the taxpayer is often asked to assist his government by producing relevant materials, but he has no guarantee that his views will be heard.

3. Triangular cases are difficult to solve. For example, if the shareholders are residents of one country, the coporation is incorporated in a second country and business is done in a third country, the resolution of conflicting tax claims may be difficult. This is primarily due to the bilateral nature of the tax-convention system. The mutual agreement procedure, which reflects the bilateral nature of that system, is not well suited for the satisfactory resolution of complicated triangular cases.
4. Even if two contracting States reach mutual agreement, it is sometimes difficult to implement. Some states have difficulties in implementing such agreements for constitutional reasons, for example if a supreme Court, or even a lower Court, has taken position in a certain case..

Proposals

In the opinion of the ICC, the rapid and equitable resolution of international tax disputes is of utmost importance for the promotion of trade and capital investments among the nations of the world. The ICC has thus devoted considerable efforts to the resolution of commercial conflicts. Given the importance of taxation in the world today the ICC thinks it is also very important that conflicts in the tax field should be resolved as rapidly and equitably as possible.

The ICC which has taken up the question of double taxation and the settlement of international tax conflict as early as 1959 therefore welcomes the growing interest in this field and the efforts made by the European Communities, the OECD and the International Fiscal Association. The ICC believes, however, that the approach to this problem has erred on the side of caution. Following years of long discussion, the time is ripe for bold initiatives in order to achieve real progress.

It is of paramount importance for the taxpayer that tax rules be clear and consistently applied. At the international level, he must be able to rely upon the texts of tax treaties. It is intolerable for the specific provisions of tax treaties not to be applied for diverse constitutional, jurisdictional or administrative reasons.

When a State has willingly limited its sovereign powers of taxation by entering into a double taxation treaty with another State, it must be deemed to have assumed full responsibility for the implementation of that treaty in each particular case.

The Mutual Agreement Procedure

The predominance of the mutual agreement procedure as a means of resolving international tax conflicts requires that measures be adopted to ensure a more efficient functioning of this procedure.

1. The taxpayer should have the right to demand the initiation of the mutual agreement procedure.
2. The taxpayer should have the right to submit any materials he wishes to the competent authorities as well as the right to be heard. He should also be authorized to put forward his views to these authorities and to be informed by them about the material aspects of the envisaged decision.
3. The mutual agreement procedure should not be used to review tax matters not directly related to the subject of the procedure.
4. A mutual agreement should be reached within a period of one year from the initiation of the procedure.
5. Once a settlement has been reached, it should be implemented irrespective of time limits in domestic law.
6. A mutual agreement should be implemented in *all* cases, even if taxation incompatible with the treaty has been confirmed by a judicial decision.
7. The taxpayer should have the right to reject any unsatisfactory mutual agreement. The remedies of national tax law should in such cases always be open to him. If the taxpayer and the competent authority so agree, the competent authority may in such a case proceed to arbitration.
8. Most important is that the competent authorities should be obliged to diligently pursue their negotiations, in such a way that double taxation is eliminated in a manner compatible with the treaty.
9. The taxpayer should be protected from paying taxes (in both States) during the mutual agreement or arbitration procedure unless domestic law provides for adequate indemnification.
10. The principles stated here should be used as much as possible even if there is no treaty.

Decision by an Independent Body

If the competent authorities are unable to reach an agreement which they find compatible with the treaty, or if they are unable to resolve the problem within one year, they should at the option of the taxpayer be obliged to submit the case to an independent body.

In the long run, the ICC thinks that it should be possible to set up an *International Tax Court*. Such a Court would have many advantages. It could set precedents and resolve cases where more than two States are involved. The position of the taxpayers would be strengthened.

The ICC recognizes, however, that many legal, practical and psychological obstacles would have to be surmounted before that state is reached. For the present, the pressing problems involved in the resolution of international tax disputes, in the event of an unsuccessful resolution of the dispute under a mutual agreement procedure, should be alleviated by the introduction of *arbitration procedures.*

1. On demand of the taxpayer, the arbitration commission should be formed by each State choosing one member, who in turn choose an impartial chairman. The chairman should be a person who inspires confidence, not only in the competent authorities, but also in the taxpayers.
2. The arbitration commission should reach a solution in conformity with the treaty. Even if its task in a particular case is primarily one of fact-finding (as in a transfer pricing case), the award should always be based on the treaty.
3. The taxpayer should have the right to present his views to the arbitration commission and put forward his arguments before meetings of the commission.
4. As in the case of the mutual agreements procedure, the award should be implemented in all cases irrespective of any time limits in domestic law, and even if taxation incompatible with the treaty has occurred as a result of a Court decision.
5. As they have not found a solution to the problems by ordinary means, the costs of the arbitration procedure should be born by the States.
6. If the interests of more than two States having treaties are involved in a particular case (triangular case), the States might choose to form a common arbitration commission for the settlement of the issue. Each State should choose one member who in turn should choose an impartial chairman. If the resulting number of members of the arbitration commission is even an additional impartial member should be chosen. The award should be based on the treaties concerned.

As background to these reflections, the ICC welcomes the fact that concrete measures for introducing arbitration procedures in transfer pricing disputes have been proposed by the institutions of the European Communities. While not wishing to endorse any particular text, the ICC expresses the hope that the European Communities will take prompt action to achieve arbitration of an effective nature, in such form as to provide in conformity with the above mentioned principles, full security against double taxation for all firms subject to taxation by EEC Member States.

The ICC has noted the position of the Committee on Fiscal Affairs of the OECD on arbitration taken in the document 'Transfer pricing, corresponding adjustments and the mutual agreement procedure' adopted on 6 July 1982. The ICC regrets that the Committee on Fiscal Affairs in this document has not been able to move forward on this issue.

www.ingramcontent.com/pod-product-compliance
Lightning Source LLC
Chambersburg PA
CBHW071353230926
51846CB00002B/539
* 9 7 8 9 0 6 5 4 4 8 6 8 2 *